INSIDE WRITING

The Academic Word List in Context

Walton Burns

SERIES DIRECTOR:
Cheryl Boyd Zimmerman

OXFORD

UNIVERSITY PRESS

198 Madison Avenue
New York, NY 10016 USA

Great Clarendon Street, Oxford, OX2 6DP, United Kingdom

Oxford University Press is a department of the University of Oxford.
It furthers the University's objective of excellence in research, scholarship,
and education by publishing worldwide. Oxford is a registered trade
mark of Oxford University Press in the UK and in certain other countries

Director, ELT New York: Laura Pearson
Head of Adult, ELT New York: Stephanie Karras
Development Editor: Rebecca Meyer
Executive Art and Design Manager: Maj-Britt Hagsted
Content Production Manager: Julie Armstrong
Design Project Manager: Michael Steinhofer
Image Manager: Trisha Masterson
Production Artist: Julie Sussman-Perez
Production Coordinator: Christopher Espejo

ISBN: 978 0 19 460106 1

Printed in China

This book is printed on paper from certified and well-managed sources

ACKNOWLEDGEMENTS

Illustration by: 5W Infographics, pgs. 2, 16, 25, Backmatter map.

*We would also like to thank the following for permission to reproduce the following
photographs*: **Cover**, David Harrigan/ableimages/Corbis; Dieter Heinemann/
Westend61/Corbis; Roger Ressmeyer/CORBIS; Odilon Dimier/PhotoAlto/
Corbis; Michelle Garrett/CORBIS; Dr. Richard Kessel & Dr. Gene Shih/
Visuals Unlimited/Corbis; Frank Krahmer / Masterfile; Jennifer Gottschalk/
shutterstock. **Interior**, p1 Michael Kraus/Shutterstock; p3 James R Clarke/
Alamy; p15 Picavet/Getty Images; p29 Sergii Tsololo/Getty Images; p30
MARK GARLICK/Science Photo Library; p31 Santiago Urquijo/Getty Images
(Earthworm); p31 the Agency Collection/Oxford University Press (astronaut);
p43 Jimmy Anderson/Getty Images; p44 Cartoonresource/shutterstock; p45
NAN728/shutterstock (Accounting); p45 Robert Kneschke/Fotolia (Woman
helping); p57 Mitrofanova/Shutterstock; p58 Chris Gramly/Getty Images;
p59 Hayati Kayhan /shutterstock (Label); p59 Sinan Isakovic/shutterstock
(Returning); p71 Julija Sapic/Shutterstock; p72 F1 ONLINE/Superstock Ltd.;
p73 Jon Arnold Images/Getty Images; p85 Karen Grigoryan/shutterstock; p86
ZEPHYR/Science Photo Library; p87 Dr. Marli Miller/Visuals Unlim/Corbis
UK Ltd; p99 Anna Hoychuk/shutterstock; p100 YAY Media AS/Alamy; p101
alex9500/Fotolia (Unsaturated fats); p101 Joe Belanger/Alamy (Fresh fruit);
p113 Africa Studio/Shutterstock; p114 Armando Capeda; p115 sima/Fotolia
(Hand painting); p115 Image Source/Alamy (Paint pots); p124 Antiquarian
Images/Alamy; p127 Allison Herreid/Shutterstock; p128 alinamd/Fotolia;
p129 Aygul Bulté/Fotolia.

Acknowledgements

We would like to acknowledge the following individuals for their input during the development of the series:

Salam Affouneh
Higher Colleges of Technology
Abu Dhabi, U.A.E.

Kristin Bouton
Intensive English Institute
Illinois, U.S.A.

Nicole H. Carrasquel
Center for Multilingual Multicultural Studies
Florida, U.S.A.

Elaine Cockerham
Higher College of Technology
Muscat, Oman

Danielle Dilkes
CultureWorks English as a Second Language Inc.
Ontario, Canada

Susan Donaldson
Tacoma Community College
Washington, U.S.A

Penelope Doyle
Higher Colleges of Technology
Dubai, U.A.E.

Edward Roland Gray
Yonsei University
Seoul, South Korea

Melanie Golbert
Higher Colleges of Technology
Abu Dhabi, U.A.E.

Elise Harbin
Alabama Language Institute
Alabama, U.S.A.

Bill Hodges
University of Guelph
Ontario, Canada

David Daniel Howard
National Chiayi University
Chiayi

Leander Hughes
Saitama Daigaku
Saitama, Japan

James Ishler
Higher Colleges of Technology
Fujairah, U.A.E.

John Iveson
Sheridan College
Ontario, Canada

Alan Lanes
Higher Colleges of Technology
Dubai, U.A.E.

Corinne Marshall
Fanshawe College
Ontario, Canada

Christine Matta
College of DuPage
Illinois, U.S.A.

Beth Montag
University at Kearney
Nebraska, U.S.A.

Kevin Mueller
Tokyo International University
Saitama, Japan

Tracy Anne Munteanu
Higher Colleges of Technology
Fujairah, U.A.E.

Eileen O'Brien
Khalifa University of Science, Technology, and Research
Sharjah, U.A.E.

Jangyo Parsons
Kookmin University
Seoul, South Korea

John P. Racine
Dokkyo Daigaku
Soka City, Japan

Scott Rousseau
American University of Sharjah
Sharjah, U.A.E.

Jane Ryther
American River College
California, U.S.A

Kate Tindle
Zayed University
Dubai, U.A.E.

Melody Traylor
Higher Colleges of Technology
Fujairah, U.A.E.

John Vogels
Higher Colleges of Technology
Dubai, U.A.E.

Kelly Wharton
Fanshawe College
Ontario, Canada

Contents

The Inside Track to Academic Success

Student Books

For additional student resources visit: www.oup.com/elt/insidewriting

iTools for all levels

The *Inside Writing* iTools is for use with an LCD projector or interactive whiteboard.

Resources for whole-class presentation

> **Book-on-screen** focuses class on teaching points and facilitates classroom management.
> **Writing worksheets** provide additional practice with the genre and Writing Models.

Resources for assessment and preparation

> Customizable Unit, Mid-term, and Final Tests evaluate student progress.
> Answer Keys

Additional instructor resources at: www.oup.com/elt/teacher/insidewriting

UNIT 1

Staying Healthy

In this unit, you will

> analyze exercise routines and how they are used on health and fitness websites.
> use explanatory writing.
> increase your understanding of the target academic words for this unit.

WRITING SKILLS

> Audience and Purpose
> Signal Words to Show Order
> **GRAMMAR** Simple Present Tense

Self-Assessment

Think about how well you know each target word, and check (✓) the appropriate column. I have…

TARGET WORDS	never seen the word before.	heard or seen the word but am not sure what it means.	heard or seen the word and understand what it means.	used the word confidently in *either* speaking or writing.
AWL				
🔑 achieve				
🔑 energy				
🔑 focus				
🔑 goal				
🔑 physical				
🔑 positive				
🔑 stress				
🔑 team				

🔑 Oxford 3000™ keywords

Building Knowledge

Read these questions. Discuss your answers in a small group.

1. Why do people exercise?

2. What kind of exercise do you do? Why?

3. What kind of exercise would you like to learn more about?

Writing Models

An exercise routine is a series of physical movements that people do to get fit or stay healthy. Read about three exercise routines posted on fitness websites.

Find the Time to Get Fit

Is it hard to find time to go to the gym or join a sports **team**? This exercise routine may be for you.

The **goal** of this routine is to help you exercise during your busy day. This routine **focuses** on making your arms and legs
5 stronger. It is also good for your heart. You do not need special equipment—only water bottles and stairs!

LIFTING WATER BOTTLES
Fill two small bottles with water. First, stand holding the bottles at your sides. Then raise your left knee and right arm out in front of you. Hold your left arm out to the side. Next, lower your
10 arms and leg. Finally, repeat, but this time raise your right knee and left arm in front of you. Hold your right arm out to the side. Repeat ten times, changing sides each time.

Lifting water bottles

STEP-UPS
Stand facing a step. Place your left foot on the step and lift yourself up. Then stand on the step with both feet. Next, step
15 back down to the ground with your left foot, and then with your right foot. Stand on the ground with both feet. Repeat. This time, start with your right foot on the step. Repeat 20 times, changing sides each time.

For the best results, do this routine three or four times a week.

Step-ups

Easy Walking

Most people quit exercise routines because they try to **achieve** too much at once. It is better to start slowly. Walking is a great way to begin to exercise.

5 The **goal** of this routine is to get you off the couch and moving. Walking gets you **physically** fit, and it can also reduce **stress**. All you need is a pair of running shoes and comfortable[1] clothes.

   • First, walk at a comfortable pace[2] for five
10   minutes. You should be able to talk easily.

   • Second, walk at a fast pace for two minutes. Talking should be difficult.

   • Third, slow down and walk at a comfortable pace for four minutes. **Focus** on breathing
15   slowly.

   • Fourth, walk fast for two minutes.

   • Finally, slow down and walk at an easy pace.

Try to walk four times a week. I am **positive** you will be ready for more **physical** activity after
20 three months.

---

[1] *comfortable:* relaxed; without pain
[2] *pace:* the speed that someone walks, runs, or moves

Get Marathon Ready

Are you already in good **physical** condition? Interval training can improve your **energy** and speed. Why not train for a marathon? Just add a watch to your running routine.

5 Running an "interval" means running at a faster pace. You are running comfortably if you can speak sentences. At your interval speed, it is difficult to talk. A "recovery interval" is slower than your comfortable speed.

First, warm up for ten minutes at an easy pace.

10 Second, begin your interval training:

   • Run at interval speed for one minute.

   • Run a two-minute recovery interval.

   • Run at a comfortable pace for five minutes.

Repeat four times.

15 Finally, walk at a comfortable pace for five minutes.

Audience and Purpose

LEARN

When you write about an exercise routine, think about your audience. Who will want to read about the routine? Also think about your purpose. Why are you writing about the routine?

Include these details in your writing:

1. The goal(s) of the exercise routine

2. A description of who the routine is for (target audience)

3. The equipment needed to do the routine

4. The health benefit(s) of doing the routine

APPLY

A. Read the exercise routines on pages 2–3 again. Answer the following questions about each routine with a partner.

1. What is the goal of each exercise routine?

   Find the Time to Get Fit: exercising on a busy day

   Easy Walking: beginning to exercise safely and slowly

   Get Marathon Ready: increase energy, train for marathon

2. Who is the routine for?

3. What equipment is needed to do each routine?

4. What are the health benefits of each routine?

B. Read about people who want a new exercise routine. Write the letter of the exercise routine that is best for each person.

   a. *Find the Time to Get Fit*
   b. *Easy Walking*
   c. *Get Marathon Ready*

_a_ 1. Jon is very busy at work. He only has 20 minutes of free time at lunch.

___ 2. Tomoko has run several 10K races. Now she wants to do a longer race.

___ 3. Maryann has tried running, but she feels sick when she runs too fast.

___ 4. Jorge does not have a lot of free time. He needs exercises that he can do quickly.

Analyze

A. Read *Easy Walking* again. Some details tell about the audience. Other details tell about the routine. Check (✓) the details that tell you about the audience.

✓ 1. Most people quit exercise routines because they try to achieve too much at once.

___ 2. All you need is a pair of running shoes and comfortable clothes.

___ 3. Second, walk at a fast pace for two minutes.

___ 4. The goal of this routine is to get you off the couch and moving.

___ 5. Try to walk four times a week.

___ 6. I am positive you will be ready for more physical activity after three months.

B. Look at the exercise routines on pages 2–3 again. Answer the questions with a partner.

1. How many exercises are there in *Find the Time to Get Fit*?

   two exercises: lifting water bottles and step-ups

2. Could you do the exercises in *Find the Time to Get Fit* without the pictures?

   _____

3. Why do you think the writer included the pictures in *Find the Time to Get Fit*?

   _____

4. How many steps are there in the "lifting water bottles" exercise? _____

5. Compare the *Finding the Time to Get Fit* routine to the *Easy Walking* routine. Which one is easier to understand? Why?

   _____

6. Is the picture in the *Get Marathon Ready* routine important? Why, or why not?

   _____

7. Of the three routines, which one is best for you? Why?

   _____

C. Look at *Get Marathon Ready* again. Discuss these questions in a small group.

1. Does the article explain where you can do this routine? Why, or why not?

2. Does it explain how often to do the routine?

3. Does it explain how many times to do the steps in the routine?

4. Do you have enough information to do this routine? Is there any other information that you think would be helpful?

Vocabulary Activities STEP I: Word Level

The noun *stress* is "a feeling of being worried." *Stress* is usually caused by a specific problem.

> *Too much homework causes* **stress** *because students feel they cannot finish it all.*

> *The soccer team felt a lot of* **stress** *before the championship game.*

The adjective *stressful* means "causing someone to feel worried."

> *It was* **stressful** *when we were losing the basketball game.*

A. Read the paragraph. Complete the sentences with *stress* or *stressful*. Compare your answers with a partner.

Preparing for an important soccer game can be (1) _____stressful_____.

First, you may worry that you will lose. This causes (2) _____.

Second, before the game, you have to practice hard. This also makes

you feel (3) _____. Finally, the end of the game is often

(4) _____. Sometimes the score is close, so anyone can win.

The noun *team* is "a group of people who play a sport together."

> *Our school has the best soccer* **team** *in the city.*

> *The national swim* **team** *won a gold medal at the international championship.*

B. Work with a partner. Use the words below to tell what kind of team each sentence describes. Take turns reading your sentences out loud.

home	national	soccer	school

1. The athletes that play for your school are called the _____school team_____.

2. A _____ needs people who can run fast.

3. The team playing in its own city or country is called the

   _____.

4. In the Olympics, your country is represented by the

   _____.

The verb *focus* means "to give all of your attention to something." As a verb, *focus* usually appears with the preposition *on*.

> *She left her job so she could **focus** on her school work.*

> *The team **focused** on preparing for its next game.*

Focus can also be a noun. The noun *focus* means "the thing that is getting a lot of attention." The noun does not appear with *on*.

> *The main **focus** of the lecture was the benefits of exercise.*

 CORPUS

C. Complete each sentence with the correct form of *focus*. Use *on* if necessary. For each sentence, write V if *focus* is used as a verb or N if *focus* is used as a noun.

__V__ 1. James turned off the television so he could _____*focus on*_____ his homework.

____ 2. Simple foods were the _____ of the healthy cooking class.

____ 3. The _____ of the next chapter is how different muscles work together.

____ 4. When she was at university, Farida _____ reaching one goal at a time.

____ 5. Safety should be the _____ of any exercise routine.

____ 6. Let's _____ the project now, so we can relax later.

D. Work with a partner. Complete the paragraph with the words in the box.

achieve	energy	focusing	goal	physically	team

Pinar wants to play a sport at her university. Her (1) _____*goal*_____

is to become a member of the university running (2) _____.

To (3) _____ her goal, she is training very hard. Pinar is

(4) _____ on running long distances. Her training is very hard

on her body—it is (5) _____ demanding. Pinar feels exhausted

after a long run. But she eats healthy food to get (6) _____

to run each day. Pinar is running longer and faster every day.

E. A *goal* is "something that you try to do or get." Work with a partner. Match the person with his or her goal. Take turns creating sentences.

_a_ 1. an English student   a. to learn English well

___ 2. a singer   b. to win a gold medal

___ 3. a salesperson   c. to have a song on the radio

___ 4. an athlete   d. to open a restaurant

___ 5. a chef   e. to sell a lot of things

1. *The goal of an English student is to learn English well.*

2. _____

3. _____

4. _____

5. _____

The adjective *positive* can mean "sure that you are correct."

> *My doctor is **positive** this exercise routine will help me get healthy.*

The adverb *positively* means "certainly" or "really" or "very."

> *He **positively** loves watching tennis. He gets up at 2 a.m. to watch matches in other countries.*

> *He is a **positively** incredible athlete. He swam 10 kilometers and then ran a marathon!*

CORPUS

F. Rewrite these sentences. Use the form of *positive* in parentheses.

1. I am certain that he will win the race. (positive)

   I am positive that he will win the race.

2. The referee really refused to change his mind. (positively)

   _____

3. We are sure that everyone can do our walking routine. (positive)

   _____

4. This new exercise routine is certainly amazing. (positively)

   _____

Grammar | Simple Present Tense

Use the simple present tense to write about facts, repeated actions, and feelings or opinions.

Exercise _makes_ you healthy.

I _play_ soccer every weekend.

She _likes_ watching tennis.

Remember to add -s or -es to the verb after _he_, _she_, or _it_. Add -s or -es to the verb after any noun or noun phrase that describes one person other than yourself.

Do not add any letters to the verb after _I_, _you_, _we_, or _they_. All plural nouns also take the base form of the verb.

A collective noun, such as _team_, uses one word to describe a group of things. Collective nouns take the same form of the verb as _he_, _she_, or _it_.

I You We They Both teams Her sisters	**run**	every morning.
He / She / It The team My sister	**runs**	

The verb _be_ has irregular forms in the present simple tense. When the noun in a sentence is yourself, and you use the word _I_, the present simple form of _be_ is _am_.

I	**am**	
You We They Some students	**are**	at the game.
He / She / It The student	**is**	

A. Read the sentences. Write the correct form of the verb in parentheses. Use the simple present tense.

1. The class (exercise) ___exercises___ every day.

2. My exercise goal (be) _____ to lose weight.

3. My brother sometimes (join) _____ me when I run.

4. You (be) _____ a better football player than I (be) _____.

5. The teacher's assistant (help) _____ me when I have trouble doing an exercise.

B. Read the letter. Complete the sentences with the simple present tense form of the verbs in parentheses.

> Hi,
>
> I _____*love*_____ soccer camp. Everything _____
>   (1. love)   (2. be)
>
> fine. So far, our team _____ the best at camp. We always
>   (3. be)
>
> _____. We won our last five games. The teams all
>   (4. win)
>
> _____ every day. The coach _____ us
>   (5. practice)   (6. help)
>
> during every practice. It's great!
>
> See you soon,
>
> Mengtian

C. Think of your favorite sport. Write sentences that tell what someone usually does in order to play that sport well. Write five sentences. Use the simple present tense.

A basketball player runs every day. _____

He or she practices throwing the ball in the basket. _____

1. _____

2. _____

3. _____

4. _____

5. _____

WRITING SKILL | Signal Words to Show Order

LEARN

When you explain an exercise routine, put the steps in chronological order. This will make the exercise routine easy for readers to understand. Use signal words to clearly tell the order of activities or events.

Signal words include ordinal number words (*first, second, third,* and so on).

First, walk at a comfortable pace for five minutes.

Second, walk at a fast pace for two minutes.

Third, slow down and walk at a comfortable pace.

Fourth, walk fast for two minutes.

Other common signal words that show order include *before, after, then, next,* and *finally.*

Before you begin, stretch your legs.

After you stretch, stand facing a step.

Then place your left foot on the step and lift yourself up.

Next, place your left foot back on the ground and step down with your right foot.

Finally, repeat the activity five times.

Use both ordinal number words and other signal words to show order and clearly explain a process.

APPLY

Read *Find the Time to Get Fit* on page 2 again. Complete the chart below with a partner. Order the activities from 1 to 4. Fill in the signal words that help you understand the order.

Activities	Order	Signal word
Then raise your left knee and right arm out in front of you. Hold your left arm out to the side.	1. ___	2. _____
First, stand holding the bottles at your sides.	3. _1_	4. _____ *First*
Finally, repeat, but this time raise your right knee and left arm in front of you.	5. ___	6. _____
Next, lower your arms and leg.	7. ___	8. _____

Collaborative Writing

A. Read the list of exercises below. With a partner, discuss the best order for these activities. Order the exercises from 1 to 7 to create your own routine. There is more than one way to order these exercises.

_____ run at a comfortable pace

_____ run backward

_____ walk

_____ stretch

_____ lift weights

_____ do step-ups

_____ run at an interval pace

B. With your partner, complete the sentences with the routine you created in activity A. You may need to change the forms of the words.

1. First, you should _____ to warm up.

2. Second, _____ for a short time.

3. Next, _____ until you feel tired.

4. Before you _____, rest and drink some water.

5. After resting, try to _____.

6. Then _____.

7. Finally, _____ to cool down.

C. Discuss the following questions with your partner.

1. Would pictures make your routine easier to understand? Why, or why not?

2. Would it be easier to understand the steps in a paragraph or in a list? Why?

3. What kind of person should do this routine?

4. What are the health benefits of doing the routine?

D. Follow the steps below to share your routine with another pair.

1. Compare the order of your activities with the order of their activities.

2. Explain why you chose your order.

3. Discuss which routine is easier to follow.

Independent Writing

A. Choose an exercise routine you can explain to others. It can be a real routine that you do regularly or a routine that you think would be helpful for your audience.

Name of routine: _____

B. Brainstorm activities in your routine and complete the idea map below. Fill in the idea map with the target audience, equipment needed, health benefits, and goals of the routine.

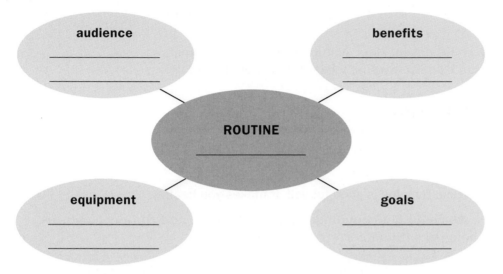

VOCABULARY TIP

Action verbs can help explain exactly how to do an exercise. Include action verbs so the instructions are easy to follow.

C. Circle the action verbs in the box that you can use in your exercise routine.

cool down	lift	pull	run	walk
hold	lower	raise	stand	warm up

D. Write an introduction that describes the goals, benefits, equipment, and audience for your routine. Complete the paragraph below as a guide.

The goal of this routine is to (1) _____.

It is best for people who (2) _____.

One benefit of the routine is that it (3) _____.

It also (4) _____. To do it, you

need (5) _____.

E. Write your exercise routine to post on a health and fitness website. Use your ideas from activities A through D. Remember to include action verbs and the target vocabulary from page 1.

REVISE AND EDIT

A. Read your explanation of an exercise routine. Answer the questions below, and make revisions to your explanation as needed.

1. Check (✓) the information you included in your explanation.

   ☐ goal of the routine

   ☐ the equipment needed

   ☐ the order of the steps

   ☐ how often to do the routine

   ☐ a description of the target audience

   ☐ health benefit(s) of the routine

   ☐ how long to do each activity

2. Look at the information you did not include. Would adding that information make your explanation of an exercise routine easier for readers to follow?

Grammar for Editing Capitalization and Punctuation

A sentence must give a complete idea or thought. Sentences always begin with a capital letter. Simple sentences end with a period (.).

> My favorite exercise is running. Running is good for you. It makes you healthy.

Avoid sentence fragments, which do not contain a complete thought, and run-on sentences, which are two complete thoughts without correct punctuation.

Sentence fragment: *My favorite exercise.*	This fragment needs a verb to finish the thought. *My favorite exercise is running.*
Run-on sentence: *My favorite exercise is running, it is good for you.*	This run-on should be two sentences. Use a period instead of a comma. Capitalize the *i* in *it*. *My favorite exercise is running. It is good for you.*

Check that your sentences give a complete thought with a noun and verb. Also, check that each sentence contains only one idea.

B. Check the language in your explanation. Revise and edit as needed.

Language Checklist
☐ I used target words in my exercise routine.
☐ I used action verbs to give clear instructions.
☐ I used the simple present tense correctly.
☐ I used complete sentences with capital letters and correct punctuation.

C. Check your explanation of an exercise routine again. Repeat activities A and B.

Self-Assessment Review: Go back to page 1 and reassess your knowledge of the target vocabulary. How has your understanding of the words changed? What words do you feel most comfortable using now?

UNIT 2

Reading the Rings

In this unit, you will

> analyze a report and see how it is used in a science magazine.
> use explanatory writing.
> increase your understanding of the target academic words for this unit.

WRITING SKILLS

> Signal Words to Connect Ideas
> Visual Aids
> **GRAMMAR** Simple Past Tense

Self-Assessment

Think about how well you know each target word, and check (✓) the appropriate column. I have…

TARGET WORDS	never seen the word before.	heard or seen the word but am not sure what it means.	heard or seen the word and understand what it means.	used the word confidently in *either* speaking or writing.
AWL				
🔑 conclude				
🔑 enormous				
🔑 expand				
🔑 major				
🔑 research				
🔑 section				
🔑 series				
🔑 visible				

🔑 Oxford 3000™ keywords

Building Knowledge

Read these questions. Discuss your answers in a small group.

1. Do you read science magazines or websites? Why, or why not?

2. What is some interesting research you have heard or read about recently?

3. Does reading about scientific research affect what you do in your daily life? Why, or why not?

Writing Model

A report tells about an event or series of events and how these events affect the world. Read about what a scientist learned from a tree.

Fire and Life: Lessons from a Tree

Recently ecologist and **researcher** William Lars studied a **section** of Yellowstone National Park in the United States. This area of the park suffered
5 an **enormous** fire in 1988. Lars wanted to **research** the effects of the fire. He discovered a very interesting Douglas fir tree. This tree did not die in the fire.

Each year, the trunk or body of a tree
10 **expands**. Each **expansion** creates one ring. The rings are **visible** only after the tree falls or is cut down. The number of rings is equal to the age of the tree. **Researchers** make **conclusions** based on the rings. They can tell how well the
15 tree grew. For example, a wide ring means the tree grew well that year. Events such as fires leave marks in the rings. Looking at the entire **series** of rings, **researchers** can understand events that affected the tree.

TREE RINGS

Bark

Forest fire

Slow growth

Strong growth

20 For example, this Douglas fir tree was planted in 1903. Lars noted a **series** of narrow rings that grew twenty-four years after the tree was planted. As a result, he believes there was a drought[1] during those years, and the tree
25 didn't have enough water to grow well.

---

[1] *drought:* a long period of time without rain or snow

However, the rings that grew after 1931 were mostly wide and even. Lars **concluded** from this that the drought ended.

Another **series** of narrow rings grew on one
30 side of the tree in 1975. From these rings, Lars **concluded** that something pushed on the tree. He thinks that other trees were probably growing too close to the fir tree. This caused overcrowding[2] and poor growth. The narrow
35 rings continued for 13 years.

Then the rings show another **major** event. A **series** of **major** fires in 1988 covered much of the forest. From this time period, the trees in the area have **visible** scars from the fire in their
40 rings. The scars look like dark, uneven marks.

Interestingly, after 1988, the rings of the Douglas fir show good growth. Lars believes the trees in the **section** around the fir tree had **major** damage. The damage caused some trees
45 to die. As a result, there were fewer trees. Because there were fewer trees, the trees that did not die could grow better.

Today wildfires are a **major** problem. People continue to look for ways to stop them from
50 happening. One **conclusion** from this report is that a fire may kill some trees, but this may help other trees to grow. In addition, when trees aren't so close together, fires can't spread as quickly. How did the Douglas fir survive the
55 fire? This will be the topic of Lars's next **research**. ■

---

[2] *overcrowding:* having too much of something; being too full

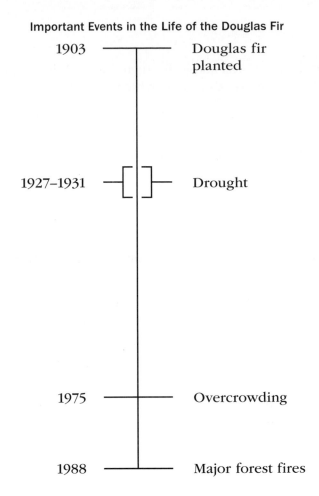

Important Events in the Life of the Douglas Fir

1903	Douglas fir planted
1927–1931	Drought
1975	Overcrowding
1988	Major forest fires

LEARN

Some signal words show the relationship between ideas. These words can show that two ideas are different, which means that they contrast. Other signal words connect events to their results, or consequences. Finally, some signal words introduce examples.

Relationship	Signal words
Contrast	I <u>like coffee</u>, **but** today I <u>am drinking tea</u>. I felt <u>tired</u> earlier. **However**, I feel <u>ready</u> to work now.
Consequence	<u>The trees are dying</u> **because** the forest is dry. We made a map of the forest. **As a result**, <u>we didn't get lost on our hike</u>.
Example	Some trees lose their leaves in the fall. **For example**, <u>the leaves of the oak tree turn brown in September and fall off in October or November</u>.

APPLY

A. Read the report on pages 16–17 again. Circle the signal words from the chart. Underline the phrases that the signal words are contrasting, connecting, or introducing.

B. Work with a partner. Write the sentence or phrase from the writing model that answers each question below.

1. What sentence or phrase contrasts with this statement?

   However, the rings that grew after 1931 were mostly wide and even.

   The tree didn't have enough water to grow well.

2. What sentence or phrase shows the consequence of this statement?

   The damage caused some trees to die.

   _____

3. What sentence has an example to support the following statements?

   Researchers make conclusions based on the rings. They can tell how well the tree grew.

   _____

4. What sentence or phrase contrasts with this idea?

   One conclusion from this report is that a fire may kill some trees.

   _____

Analyze

A. Read the first paragraph of the report on page 16 again. Circle the correct answer to each question below. Discuss your answers with a partner.

1. What is the topic of this report?

   (a.) a Douglas fir tree

   b. Yellowstone National Park

   c. Lars, an interesting researcher

2. Where did Lars do his research?

   a. a fir tree farm

   b. Yellowstone National Park

   c. the U.S. Fire Safety Department

3. What was the purpose of Lars's research?

   a. to map Yellowstone National Park

   b. to learn why fires start

   c. to understand the effects of fire

4. What interesting thing did Lars find?

   a. an enormous fire in Yellowstone National Park

   b. a Douglas fir tree that did not die in the fire

   c. the effects of geography on a forest fire

B. Reports tell facts and explain conclusions based on those facts. Match each description of tree rings with a conclusion. Compare your answers with a partner.

Fact	Conclusion
_b_ 1. wide, even rings	a. other trees pushed against the tree
___ 2. narrow rings	b. healthy growth
___ 3. narrow rings on only one side	c. not enough water
___ 4. a dark, uneven mark	d. fire

C. Read the last paragraph of the report on page 17 again. Check (✓) the statements below that describe situations where this research might be useful. Explain your choices to a partner.

_✓_ 1. a forest in Canada where fires spread quickly every year

___ 2. a national park in Spain that wants to plant more trees

___ 3. a hiking area where campers often cook food over fires

___ 4. an overcrowded forest in northern Mongolia

___ 5. a city planner designing a park

Vocabulary Activities STEP I: Word Level

A. Complete the chart below with the correct forms of the target words. Use a dictionary to check your answers.

conclude	conclusion	expand	expansion	research	researcher

Word Form Chart	
Noun	**Verb**
conclusion	

B. Complete the paragraph below using the correct forms of the words from activity A. Change the tense of the verbs if necessary.

Today a famous (1) _____researcher_____ who studies animals in city

environments spoke at the university. She spent the last year doing

(2) _____ on the effect of flooding on city animals. She studied

a city park that had a small river. After heavy rains, the river got bigger. It

(3) _____ until it was two times wider than usual. After studying

the park for a year, she (4) _____ that the river's expansion made

it harder for some animals to find food.

Something that is *visible* is something that you can see.

   *After the fire, burn marks were **visible** on the trees.*

The opposite adjective, *invisible*, describes things that you cannot see.

   *Many animals are so small that they are **invisible** without a microscope.*

CORPUS

C. Read each noun below. Write *visible* if you can see it, or *invisible* if you cannot see it.

_____invisible_____ 1. clean air

_____ 2. a painting

_____ 3. fire

_____ 4. a song

Vocabulary Activities   STEP II: Sentence Level

Major is an adjective that means "important or large."

*The plants and animals are a **major** reason people visit this park.*

As a noun, *major* means "the main subject that you study at college." Most of your classes are on that subject.

*My **major** was electrical engineering.*

The noun *majority* refers to "the largest part of something." Use the preposition *of* after *majority*.

*The **majority** of people in Germany prefer coffee to tea.*

CORPUS

D. Rewrite the sentences below using the form of *major* in parentheses.

1. That forest is an important home of evergreen trees. (major)

   That forest is a major home of evergreen trees.
   _____

2. I'm studying biology because I love science and nature. (major)

   _____

   _____

3. People are a large cause of forest fires. (major)

   _____

4. Most people believe parks, forests, and other green spaces are important. (majority)

   _____

The noun *series* means "a number of things of the same kind that happen one after another."

*A **series** of articles about gardening will appear in the newspaper every Tuesday for one month.*

A *series* often refers to "a set of television shows."

*I never miss my favorite television **series**. It is on Channel 7 every Sunday at 8 p.m.*

The noun *section* is "a part of something."

*I always read the sports **section** of the newspaper first, and then the entertainment **section**.*

CORPUS

E. Work with a partner. Write S next to each item below that is a series of things, and write C next to each item that is a section of something. Take turns making sentences describing the items. Use *series* or *section* in your sentences.

_S_ 1. a weekly television drama

A weekly television drama is a series such as Downton Abbey.

_C_ 2. the part of the library where DVDs are kept

The media section is where DVDs are kept.

___ 3. the part of the park with playgrounds

_____

___ 4. three soccer games played by the same two teams

_____

___ 5. four interviews with famous authors

_____

___ 6. the last paragraph of an essay

_____

___ 7. part of a textbook that is about protecting nature

_____

F. Answer each question below. Use one of the target words in the box.

enormous	major	visible

1. What is the biggest animal you have ever seen?

   I saw an elephant in the zoo. It was enormous.

2. What is the smallest thing you can see with your eyes?

   _____

3. What subject did you focus on in college? Or what subject will you focus on?

   _____

Grammar Simple Past Tense

Use the simple past tense to talk about something that happened in the past.

Form the simple past tense by adding -*ed* to the base form of regular verbs.

> Lars *wanted* to research the effects of the fire.

> For example, the Douglas fir tree that Lars *researched* was *planted* in 1903.

Some verbs have different spellings in the past tense, in addition to adding -*ed*.

stop	→	stopped
study	→	studied
say	→	said

Form a negative statement by using *did not* + base form of the verb. You can also use the contraction *didn't*.

> The tree *did not die* in the fire.

> He *didn't* see any signs of damage in other trees.

A. Read the report on pages 16–17 again. Work with a partner. Circle four simple past tense verbs in the first paragraph of the report. Write the base form of each verb below.

   study
   _____

   _____

   _____

   _____

B. Complete the paragraph below. Write the simple past tense of each verb in parentheses.

My friend and I _____*wanted*_____ to take a fun trip last year. My sister
             (1. want)

_____ to go to Mongolia, so that's what we did! However, my
    (2. say)

friend and I _____ in a hotel. We _____ in a special tent
       (3. not stay)   (4. live)

called a yurt for two weeks. We _____ our food over a fire and
                       (5. cook)

_____ many interesting things to eat. We _____ through
    (6. try)   (7. hike)

the prairie and _____ to the capital city. We also _____ a
       (8. travel)   (9. meet)

lot of friendly people everywhere we _____.
                        (10. go)

C. Work with a partner. Ask and answer the questions below.

1. Did you watch television last night?

   Yes, I watched a movie on TV last night.

   No, I didn't watch TV last night.

2. Where did you study last year?

   _____

3. Where did you travel the last time you took a trip?

   _____

4. What did you learn in class yesterday?

   _____

5. What games did you play when you were a child?

   _____

6. Who helped you learn English?

   _____

WRITING SKILL | Visual Aids

LEARN

A visual aid is a picture, illustration, diagram, map, chart, graph, or other item that gives an audience information they can see instead of read. Authors use visual aids to help explain their writing.

A diagram is a picture or illustration that shows how something works or what something looks like. Diagrams need a title, and the different parts must be labeled.

Diagram of Tree Rings

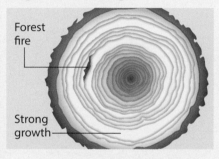

A map is a drawing of part of the earth's surface that shows countries, rivers, mountains, roads, or other features. Maps need to be clearly labeled.

A timeline is a line that is marked and labeled to show the order in which past events happened.

Important Events in the Life of the Douglas Fir Tree

Charts and graphs organize information using pictures and show relationships between things. Charts and graphs are best for showing numbers and amounts of things. They need to be clearly labeled.

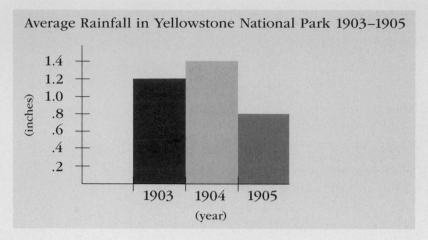

Average Rainfall in Yellowstone National Park 1903–1905

APPLY

A. Read the report on pages 16–17 again. For each event listed on the timeline on page 17, underline the description that gives the same information in the writing model. Then answer the questions below.

1. What is the title of the timeline? _____

2. How many events are on the timeline? _____

B. Look at the diagram on page 16. Answer the questions below.

1. What is the title of the diagram? _____

2. What labels does the diagram have? _____

3. What information from the report does it explain? _____

Collaborative Writing

A. Discuss the questions below with a partner.

1. Do the visual aids on pages 16 and 17 help you understand the report? Why, or why not?

2. Why do you think the author chose these two types of visual aids?

B. Work with your partner. Look at the information below. Write the name of the type of visual aid that would best show the information.

1. The average rainfall in Yellowstone National Park was 0.2 inches in 1927; 0.3 in 1928; 0.1 in 1929; and 0.2 in 1930. _____

2. The section of Yellowstone National Park that suffered enormous fires in 1988 stretched from Grant Village to West Yellowstone and included most of the forests west of Yellowstone Lake. _____

C. Work in a group of four. Choose information from activity B and draw a visual aid to show it. Include a title for your visual aid and any labels or other information needed.

D. Share your visual aid with the class. Discuss these questions:

1. Does the visual aid show the information correctly?

2. Is this the best type of visual aid for showing the information? Why, or why not?

3. Does the visual aid help readers understand the information? Why, or why not?

Independent Writing

A. Choose a place you know well. You will write a short report about the history of that place. You may want to write about the changes in your neighborhood, city, park, home, or other area you know well.

Place: _____

B. Brainstorm the major events and changes. List them on the timeline below to organize your ideas.

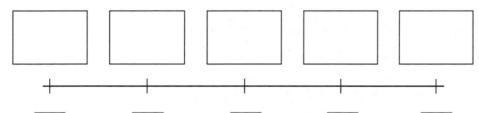

C. Use signal words to connect facts from your timeline with conclusions about those facts. Complete the sentences below as a guide.

_____

because _____.

_____,

and as a result, _____.

Because of this, _____.

For example, _____.

D. What visual aids would help your readers understand your report? Would a map of the area help readers picture your description? Would a diagram better explain your details? Draw a visual aid to include in your report. Give it a title and label the important details.

E. Write your report. Use events from your timeline in activity B to help you. Include your conclusions about the events and your visual aid. Use the target vocabulary from page 15 and connect your ideas with signal words.

A. Read your report. Answer the questions below, and make revisions to your report as needed.

1. Check (✓) the information you included in your report.

   ☐ introduction of topic   ☐ description of events

   ☐ purpose of the report   ☐ facts and conclusions

   ☐ location or name of place   ☐ visual aid

2. Look at the information you did not include. Would adding that information make your report easier to understand?

Grammar for Editing | Irregular Verbs in the Simple Past

Some verbs have irregular forms in the simple past tense. You cannot put them into the past tense by only adding -*ed*.

The verb *to be* is irregular. It has two forms: *was* and *were*.

> I *was* a student 20 years ago.   They *were* my teachers when I was young.

Here are other common irregular verbs:

Verb	Past form	Verb	Past form	Verb	Past form
begin	began	get	got	leave	left
come	came	go	went	make	made
do	did	have	had	see	saw
eat	ate	know	knew	write	wrote

B. Check the language in your report. Revise and edit as needed.

Language Checklist
☐ I used target words in my report.
☐ I used signal words to connect ideas.
☐ I used the simple past tense to describe events in the past.
☐ I correctly spelled all irregular verbs in the simple past tense.

C. Check your report again. Repeat activities A and B.

Self-Assessment Review:
Go back to page 15 and reassess your knowledge of the target vocabulary. How has your understanding of the words changed? What words do you feel most comfortable using now?

UNIT 3

Life in Space

In this unit, you will

> analyze a magazine article and see how it is used to explain biology research.
> use predictive writing.
> increase your understanding of the target academic words for this unit.

WRITING SKILLS

> Predictions and Facts
> Topic Sentences
> **GRAMMAR** Future Tense

Self-Assessment

Think about how well you know each target word, and check (✓) the appropriate column. I have…

TARGET WORDS	never seen the word before.	heard or seen the word but am not sure what it means.	heard or seen the word and understand what it means.	used the word confidently in *either* speaking or writing.
AWL				
🔑 adapt				
🔑 data				
🔑 design				
🔑 final				
🔑 job				
🔑 normal				
🔑 predict				
🔑 require				

🔑 Oxford 3000™ keywords

Building Knowledge

Read these questions. Discuss your answers in a small group.

1. Would you like to travel to space? Why, or why not?

2. Do you think people will travel to Mars someday?

3. Do you like to read about science?

Writing Model

An article appears in a newspaper, magazine, or online. Articles make an interesting topic simple for a wide audience to understand. Read an article about worms in space.

Worms in Space

By Mina Yu

Sending people to Mars is an exciting goal, but what about worms? Yes, worms—those long, thin animals that live in the ground. Surprisingly, they are probably going
5 to go to Mars before we do.

Why worms? Mars is 225,000,000 kilometers from Earth. To go there, we will have to fly for at least eight months. However, there are many things we don't know. Traveling in space for
10 such a long time might not be safe for humans. Sending worms first is a less dangerous way to collect **data**. With that information, scientists can test three **predictions** about how well people can survive[1] the long journey to Mars.
15 For example, scientists **predict** that people will lose too much muscle being in space for such a long period of time. On Earth, gravity holds us to the planet. Human beings **require** strong muscles to move against gravity. But
20 there is no gravity in space. Astronauts don't

---

[1] *survive:* to stay alive during a difficult or dangerous time

need to use as much muscle power to move. As a result, their muscles become smaller and weaker. Some astronauts never get back all their muscle after they return to Earth. This is a serious health problem. On the other hand, human beings may be able to **adapt** and keep their muscles strong while they're in space. That would make travel in space less dangerous. Scientists can watch the worms to collect **data** about muscle weakening.

Scientists also worry about the health risks[2] of radiation. Radiation is a form of energy similar to X-rays that some substances[3] send out. Some people have gotten cancer from it. There may be dangerous radiation in space that is not **normally** found on Earth. However, people can **adapt** to different environmental conditions as well. Space-traveling worms will provide scientists with more **data** about what the radiation levels in space can do to an animal that is meant to live on Earth.

Finally, astronauts **require** food and water. The trip to Mars is very long. Carrying enough

food will definitely be expensive. Scientists **predict** that people are going to grow their own food in space, as they do on Earth. If worms can survive well in space, maybe animals **normally** used for food can as well.

There is still a lot to learn. Scientists have a large **job** ahead to **design** further experiments. But the Mars project has already begun. Believe it or not, someday we will **finally** reach Mars. And we will have worms to thank.

---

[2] *health risk:* the possibility that something bad may happen to your health
[3] *substance:* a basic material; any solid, liquid, or gas

Predictions and Facts

LEARN

A prediction is someone's opinion about what will happen in the future. Predictions may or may not actually happen. Sentences that describe facts refer to things that are true in the present. Most predictions about the future are based on facts in the present.

Predictions often use the future tense:

> We **will** travel to Mars one day.

> It**'s going to** rain tomorrow.

Facts are usually stated in the present tense. This can be the simple present, or the present progressive using *be* + base form of the verb + *-ing*.

> People **need** food to survive.

> Scientists **are designing** new rockets.

When you write predictions, it is better to support your prediction by including facts. Giving facts or reasons makes your prediction stronger. Facts show *why* you believe the prediction will come true.

prediction | fact

Humans will travel to Mars someday. Scientists are already researching how to make it safe for astronauts by studying worms in space.

fact | prediction

Companies already make and test planes that go to space. Someday, people are going to fly in space on private spaceships.

APPLY

A. Read the article on pages 30–31 again. Underline the eight sentences that contain the future tense. Write them in the chart in activity B. Check (✓) the ones that are predictions. Compare your answers with a partner.

B. With your partner, find the fact in the article that supports each prediction below. The fact might appear before or after the prediction. Write the fact in the chart.

	Sentence in future tense	Prediction?	Supporting fact
1.	*Surprisingly, they are probably going to go to Mars before we do.*	✓	*Sending worms first is a less dangerous way to collect data.*
2.	*To go there, we will have to fly for at least eight months.*		
3.			
4.			
5.			
6.			
7.			
8.			

Analyze

A. Read the article on pages 30–31 again and fill in the outline below with the three main predictions the scientists want to test. List the predictions and the reasons (facts) that support the predictions. Compare your answers with a partner.

Paragraph 3

I. Prediction: *Muscle loss will be a big problem.*

    Reasons:

      1. *There is no gravity in space.*

      2. *Without gravity we can lose muscle.*

Paragraph 4

II. Prediction: _____

    Reasons:

       1. _____

       2. _____

Paragraph 5

III. Prediction: _____

    Reason: _____

B. Look at the reasons you listed in activity A. Circle the best answer to each of the following questions. Compare your answers with a partner.

1. Why does the author mention gravity in paragraph 3?

    (a.) to explain why astronauts lose muscles in space

    b. to show how scientists predict worms will move in space

2. Why does the author mention that radiation can cause cancer in paragraph 4?

    a. to give an example of how people can adapt

    b. to show why radiation can be dangerous

3. Why does the author talk about growing food in space in paragraph 5?

    a. to explain why worms are being sent into space

    b. to give an example of why carrying food is expensive

C. Work with a partner. Find the scientific words listed below in the article on pages 30–31. Write the definition from the article. Then answer the questions below with a partner.

gravity: _____

radiation: _____

1. Did you know the meaning of these words before you read the article?

2. Is this article written for scientists? Explain your answer.

Vocabulary Activities   STEP I: Word Level

The verb *design* means "to create a plan that shows how to make something."

    *Scientists will **design** a spaceship that can protect astronauts from radiation.*

A *designer* is "a person who designs things."

    *The **designer** added straps to the chairs so astronauts will stay in them without gravity.*

A. Match the type of designer in the box with what that person designs. Discuss your answers with a partner. Use a dictionary if necessary.

architect	furniture designer	landscape architect
fashion designer	jewelry designer	web designer

1. houses: _____architect_____

2. websites: _____

3. tables: _____

4. dresses: _____

5. gardens: _____

6. earrings: _____

B. A *job* is work that you do regularly to earn money. It is often a title of a paid position, such as *salesperson* or *teacher*. Check (✓) the following phrases that might be considered a job. Discuss your choices with a partner.

✓ 1. working as a nurse in a hospital

___ 2. sweeping the floor

___ 3. riding a train

___ 4. making copies of a report before a meeting

___ 5. playing with a child

___ 6. driving a taxi

C. Complete the chart below with the correct forms of the target words *data*, *predict*, and *require*. Use a dictionary to check your answers.

Word Form Chart		
Noun	**Verb**	**Adjective**
	_____	_____
	require	
	predict	_____

D. Complete each sentence below with the correct form of the word *data*, *predict*, or *require*.

1. Physical fitness is just one of the ____requirements____ for becoming an astronaut.

2. What kind of food will worms _____ in space?

3. Scientists collected _____ by measuring how much the worms grew.

4. Scientists are using worms to _____ how human muscles will react to long periods of time spent in space.

5. We will load all of the _____ supplies onto the spaceship.

6. Their conclusions are based on large amounts of _____.

To *adapt* means "to change in some way for a new or different situation." In this meaning, it often appears with the word *to*.

*The scientists had to **adapt** <u>to</u> the extreme cold at the South Pole.*

To *adapt* can also mean "to change something so you can use it in a different way." In this meaning, it often appears with *for*.

*My friend wants to **adapt** his car <u>for</u> racing.*

The noun form is *adaptation*.

*Worms developed several **adaptations** <u>to</u> living in space.*

E. Work with a partner. Rewrite the sentences below using the form of the word *adapt* in parentheses. Use *to* or *for*.

1. Humans are good at being in new places. (adapting)

   Humans are good at adapting to new places.

2. They redesigned the spaceship so that it would be able to fly faster. (adapted)

   _____

3. One change was making the spaceship longer and thinner. (adaptation)

   _____

4. The astronauts got used to living in smaller spaces. (adapted)

   _____

5. The scientists had to change their design when a longer trip was planned. (adapt)

   _____

Final is an adjective that means "last."

*This is our **final** class before the summer break.*

The noun *finals* is a plural noun that means "exams at the end of a school term."

*I'm studying hard for my **finals** so I can graduate.*

F. In a small group, write a sentence about what probably happened before each event below. Use the words in parentheses in your answers.

1. The student graduated from college. (her finals)

   The student passed her finals.
   _____

2. The championship team celebrated. (final game)

   _____
   _____

3. Parliament passed the law. (final vote)

   _____
   _____

4. The pianist bowed and the audience applauded. (final song)

   _____
   _____

G. Work with a partner. Think of a job. Answer the following questions to describe this job. Use the words in **bold** in your answers. Share your answers with another pair. Guess which job they are describing.

The job title: _____

1. Who will like doing this **job**? *A person who likes helping people will like this job.*

2. What is a **normal** task for this job? _____

3. What skills does this job **require**? _____

4. What do you **predict** will be hard about the job? _____

Grammar Future Tense

To write about the future, use *will* or *be going to*.

Use *will* to write about predictions based on your opinion.

> By the year 2500, people _will live_ in space.

Use *will* for a promise you make.

> I _will call_ you tonight.

Use *be going to* for predictions based on something that just happened or is happening now.

> There are a lot of clouds outside. It _is going to rain_.

Use *be going to* to write about plans.

> I _am going to take_ classes in astronomy. I already talked to the professor.

Form the negative by adding *not* to both forms.

> We _will not_ travel to another solar system.

> We _are not going to_ eat at this restaurant again.

A. Read the paragraph below. Circle the correct form of the verbs in parentheses. Use *be going to* for things that are already planned, and *will* for things that are not known yet.

Researchers (1) (are going to conduct)/ will conduct) an experiment next week. They (2) (are going to test / will test) how people (3) (are going to react / will react) to traveling in space alone. They do not know if it (4) (is going to be / will be) hard to be alone for a long time. The experiment was carefully designed. One person (5) (is going to live / will live) in a tiny room for one month. Scientists think it (6) (is going to be / will be) very stressful.

B. Complete each sentence below with one predication about what you think will happen and one prediction about what you think will not happen. Use *be going to* if you already have plans. Share your answers with a partner.

1. Tomorrow,

   I am going to watch a movie.

   I am not going to do homework.

2. Next week,

   _____

   _____

3. Next year,

   _____

   _____

4. In ten years,

   _____

   _____

WRITING SKILL   Topic Sentences

LEARN

A well-written paragraph has one main idea. Everything in the paragraph is connected to the main idea. The main idea is usually expressed in one sentence called a *topic sentence*. A clear topic sentence helps the reader understand the whole paragraph.

In this paragraph, the topic sentence is the first sentence.

> *According to a new report, exercise helps us study better. Researchers followed students who were preparing for a test. Half of them exercised for one hour every day. The other half studied for an extra hour. Surprisingly, the students who exercised did better on the test. This may be because exercise helps students relieve stress. Maybe exercise helps the brain work better. In any case, students need to both study and work out to do well.*

The paragraph is about exercise and studying. These two words are repeated many times. Only the topic sentence clearly explains the relationship between exercise and studying, without giving details. The other sentences in the paragraph contain details that support or explain this idea.

APPLY

Write each topic sentence in the box below at the beginning of the correct paragraph. One of the sentences will not be used.

> ~~Traveling anywhere in space takes a long time.~~
> It is very expensive to pay for a space program.
> Traveling in space will become a normal activity in the future.
> Traveling in space may be very difficult for people.
> There are a lot of dangers to sending people into space.

_____*Traveling anywhere in space takes a long time.*_____ Scientists predict it will take eight to ten months to get to Mars. Going to another galaxy could take years. Traveling to the moon only takes four days, but we have already researched the moon. All of the more interesting places are farther away.

_____ The launch, when the rocket leaves the ground, is the most dangerous part. The fuel used in rockets can explode or catch on fire. Also, there is a lot of equipment on a spaceship. If one thing goes wrong, it can lead to serious problems.

_____ Last year, the United States spent almost two billion dollars on space travel. Russia spent closer to five billion dollars. You need well-trained people and a lot of special equipment. Traveling to space is not simple, so the cost is quite high.

_____ First of all, it is frightening to be going so far from home. Second, you are in a very small space. Third, there is a lot of work to be done. So it can be a very stressful experience.

Collaborative Writing

A. Look at the notes for a paragraph predicting a potential problem with long space journeys. Write a topic sentence for this paragraph.

> Topic sentence: _____
> - spaceship = small
> - crew = 4–6 people
> - problems:
> 1. conflicts – no privacy, no place to be alone
> 2. boredom – small space, no fun

B. With a partner, look at the notes in activity A again. Complete the sentences below to make predictions and state facts for this new paragraph.

1. Traveling in a spaceship is not normal because

_____.

2. Living with four to six people in a small space requires

_____.

3. I predict conflicts can start because

_____.

4. Astronauts should adapt to

_____.

C. Work with a partner. Use the notes in activity A and your sentences from activity B to write a paragraph predicting a problem with long-term space travel.

D. Share your paragraph with another pair. Discuss the questions below.

1. Is there a clear topic sentence in each paragraph?

2. What differences are there between the paragraphs?

3. Do those differences make one paragraph better than the other? If so, how?

4. What do you like about the other pair's paragraph?

Independent Writing

A. You are going to write a paragraph predicting what life will be like in space. Complete the outline below with two predictions about life in space. Provide at least one reason why you believe each prediction will happen. Your reasons may be facts or examples.

I. Prediction:

_____

Reasons

1. _____

2. _____

II. Prediction:

_____

Reasons

1. _____

2. _____

B. Think about each prediction from activity A. How sure are you that it is true? Add an adverb to each prediction to describe how sure you are that it will happen.

C. Write a topic sentence for your paragraph. Complete the sentences below as a guide.

I predict that in space we will _____ because

_____.

There will also be _____ because in space there is

_____.

VOCABULARY TIP

Use adverbs such as *definitely, probably, possibly,* or *maybe* to show how likely a prediction is to come true.

D. Write your paragraph. Use your outline from activity A and ideas from activity C. In your writing, use the target vocabulary on page 29 and include adverbs to show how likely you think your predictions are to happen.

REVISE AND EDIT

A. Read your paragraph. Answer the questions below, and make revisions to your paragraph as needed.

1. Check (✓) the information you included in your paragraph.

   ☐ predictions   ☐ facts

   ☐ examples   ☐ consequences

2. Look at the information you did not include. Would adding that information make your paragraph easier to understand?

Grammar for Editing | Parts of Speech

To be complete, a sentence needs a subject and verb.

A subject can be a noun, pronoun, or proper noun. Use the pronouns *I, you, he/she/it, we,* or *they* as the subject in sentences. A proper noun names a specific person or thing. Always capitalize a proper noun.

                                       pronoun   proper noun

noun   verb   ⌐⌐ verb   ⌐⌐ verb

Teachers work in a school. On Wednesdays, he works at a bakery. Khoi works in a hospital.

The subject can be one word or a group of words.

  subject   subject   subject

The beach is a pleasant place. You and I are very busy. The country of France is in Europe.

B. Check the language in your paragraph. Revise and edit as needed.

Language Checklist
☐ I used target words in my paragraph.
☐ I used adverbs to show how likely my predictions are to come true.
☐ I used the future tense correctly.
☐ I used parts of speech correctly in complete sentences.

C. Check your paragraph again. Repeat activities A and B.

Self-Assessment Review: Go back to page 29 and reassess your knowledge of the target vocabulary. How has your understanding of the words changed? What words do you feel most comfortable using now?

UNIT 4

What Should I Do?

In this unit, you will

> analyze personal narratives and how they are used in periodicals.
> use problem-and-solution organization.
> increase your understanding of the target academic words for this unit.

WRITING SKILLS

> Problem-Solution Organization
> Supporting Details
> **GRAMMAR** *There Is/There Are*

Self-Assessment

Think about how well you know each target word, and check (✓) the appropriate column. I have...

TARGET WORDS	never seen the word before.	heard or seen the word but am not sure what It means.	heard or seen the word and understand what it means.	used the word confidently in *either* speaking or writing.
AWL				
🔑 accurate				
🔑 assist				
🔑 error				
🔑 individual				
🔑 initial				
🔑 objective				
🔑 relax				
🔑 resource				

🔑 Oxford 3000™ keywords

Building Knowledge

Read these questions. Discuss your answers in a small group.

1. Would a class about solving problems in society be interesting to you? Why, or why not?

2. Do you know what career you want? How did you choose it?

3. What advice would you give to someone choosing a career?

Writing Model

A personal narrative is a story about a problem in the writer's life. Read about a woman who made a difficult choice about her career.

Making Choices

How do you decide on a career? Do you really know at age 18 what you want to do with your life? When I entered college, I had a clear **objective**. I wanted to be an accountant.[1] In high
5 school, I had a job at an insurance business. I **assisted** in simple record keeping and office organization. There is a need to be very **accurate** in accounting, and I was. By the time I entered college, I was doing more advanced math and
10 accounting work. I made very few **errors**. I thought I had found the perfect career for me. However, I started to feel differently about my choice.

Initially, I enjoyed my college classes. In fact,
15 there was a sociology class that I loved. I was discussing and learning so many new and interesting things. We read about cities and organization. We discussed the **resources** people in a city need to live well. There were real

---

[1] *accountant:* a person whose job is to keep or examine the financial records of a business

problems to solve for real **individuals**. But then my sociology class ended. I took more and more advanced math and business courses. I started to feel bored. I began to make **errors**. I wished I were still in my sociology class. But I was focused on my **objective** of becoming an accountant.

Then fall break[2] came. I finally had some time to **relax**. I talked to my older brother. He saw how excited I was about my sociology class. I also told him about my accounting classes. I wasn't doing well in them, but I was scared to change my major. What if sociology wasn't right, either?

He gave me some advice. Years later, I still remember it. He said, "Sometimes there is no right answer, but you have to make a choice. Make the best choice you can." I thought about my interests. I talked to my sociology professor and my manager at work. Both said that I was skilled in math.

I made my choice and graduated with a master's degree in sociology. Now I am a social worker. I use math in my job, but mainly I work with people. I help them with their problems. I often give my brother's advice.

---

[2] *break:* a period of rest

Accounting

Sociology

LEARN

In personal narratives, writers describe a problem from their life and tell about the solution. Many magazines publish personal narratives. Readers enjoy learning how someone else solved a problem. Problem-solution writing in a personal narrative often follows this organization:

1. Background events: The writer describes events needed to understand the problem.

2. Problem: The writer describes the problem and his or her feelings about it.

3. Solution: The writer tells how he or she solved the problem.

4. Conclusion: The writer describes his or her life now that the problem is solved.

APPLY

A. Read the personal narrative on pages 44–45 again. Match each statement below to its place in the narrative's organization. You will use one letter twice.

    a. Background Event
    b. Problem
    c. Solution
    d. Conclusion

_a_ 1. In high school, I had a job at an insurance business.

___ 2. "Make the best choice you can."

___ 3. In fact, there was a sociology class that I loved.

___ 4. I use math in my job, but mainly I work with people.

___ 5. What if sociology wasn't right, either?

B. Write the statements from activity A in the correct order below.

1. _In high school, I had a job at an insurance business._

2. _____

3. _____

4. _____

5. _____

Analyze

A. In personal narratives, the writer uses different techniques to make the story interesting. Match each statement to the writer's purpose.

> a. to tell exactly what someone said
>
> b. to ask readers to think about their own lives
>
> c. to describe a feeling
>
> d. to describe an event

_b_ 1. How do you decide on a career?

____ 2. "Sometimes there is no right answer."

____ 3. There was a sociology class that I loved.

____ 4. We read about cities and organization.

B. People may read personal narratives to find solutions to their own problems. Check (✓) the people below that this personal narrative might help. Discuss the reasons for your answers with a partner.

_✓_ 1. a student who can't decide what to study in college

____ 2. a person who is happy in a new job

____ 3. a young person looking for a job

____ 4. someone who is having trouble making a decision

____ 5. a person with a job who wants to go back to school and change careers

C. Read the narrative on pages 44–45 again. Answer these questions with a partner.

1. What is the writer's purpose of the first paragraph?

   a. to give a reason why she chose a career in accounting

   b. to explain why she chose a career in sociology

   c. to introduce her reasons for changing her career choice

2. How many paragraphs give background information? _____

3. How many paragraphs give the solution? _____

4. Why do you think the writer included more background information

   than solutions? _____

   _____

D. Discuss these questions in a small group.

1. Do you think the writer is happy with her choice? Why, or why not?

2. Read the quotation in the third paragraph again. Why do you think the writer includes what her brother tells her?

3. In the last paragraph, the writer gives some details about her life now. Why do you think she includes this information?

Vocabulary Activities STEP I: Word Level

The adjective *accurate* means "correct" or "to have no mistakes."

> *I made sure my information was **accurate** and complete.*

If you do something *accurately*, you do it without making mistakes. The noun form is *accuracy*.

A. Complete each sentence below with the correct form of *accurate* or *error*.

1. Please use a dictionary to be sure that your essay does not have spelling
   _____*errors*_____.

2. Looking back, I feel that it was an _____ to choose a career when I was so young.

3. As a journalist, Farida's job is to report the news _____ every day.

4. The magazine apologized for an _____ in one of its articles.

5. Career coaches try to give students an _____ idea of what it is like to work in different professions.

6. The football player was famous for the _____ of his aim when he kicked the ball.

A *resource* is "something that a person or group of people can use for help when needed." It can refer to different things that provide something valuable.

> *Most of the world's energy comes from natural **resources** such as oil and gas.*

resources = oil and gas

> *The DVD that came with my book is a great learning **resource**.*

resource = DVD

B. Work with a partner. Use the words below to form collocations that describe each type of resource. Use a dictionary to look up any unfamiliar words.

energy	financial	learning	teaching	water

1. The new school is going to have a wonderful library. Students will have

   so many _____*learning resources*_____.

2. Oil and gas are examples of _____.

3. A country's _____ include rivers and lakes.

4. My professor uses videos, slideshow presentations, and podcasts. He has a lot

   of great _____.

5. The company does not have enough money to buy everyone a new computer.

   It has very few _____.

C. Complete the chart below with the correct forms of the target words *initial* and *individual*. Use a dictionary to check your answers.

Word Form Chart			
Noun	**Verb**	**Adjective**	**Adverb**
		initial	
	_____		individually

D. Complete each sentence below with the correct form of *initial* or *individual*.

Last year I moved from an apartment to a neighborhood with houses, where

each home is in an (1) _____*individual*_____ building. (2) _____, I did

not like it. I missed living close to other (3) _____. I told a friend

about my problem, and she advised me not to rely on my (4) _____

impression. So I invited some neighbors over for dinner. Once I got to know

them (5) _____, I realized there were a lot of friendly people in my

new neighborhood.

To *relax* means "to rest and to be calm."

*After a long day of work, Ahmed likes to **relax** by watching TV.*

CORPUS

E. With a partner, discuss which of the activities are *relaxing*. Take turns explaining your reasons. Then complete the sentence to explain your choice.

Going to the movies is relaxing because I enjoy watching an interesting story _____.

or

Going to the movies is not relaxing because I don't like how loud movie theaters are _____.

1. Eating in a park is _____ because

   _____.

2. Reading a book is _____ because

   _____.

3. Drinking coffee or tea with a friend is _____ because

   _____.

4. Exercising is _____ because

   _____.

5. Cooking dinner is _____ because

   _____.

6. Long train or bus rides are _____ because

   _____.

7. Playing sports is _____ because

   _____.

F. Circle the informal word with the same meaning as each formal target word. Then rewrite the informal sentences. Replace each synonym with the correct target word to make the sentence more formal. Finish each sentence with your own details.

Formal target word	Informal synonym
assistance	1. (stop / (help) / demand)
error	2. (task / statement / mistake)
initial	3. (first / negative / agree)
objective	4. (calendar / hobby / goal)

5. I need your help ...

   I need your assistance with this project.

6. I need to correct the mistakes ...

   _____

7. My first reaction was surprise when ...

   _____

8. Our goal is to sell ....

   _____

G. Imagine your friend is having problems learning another language. Give him or her advice. Use the phrases below in your sentences.

1. accurate vocabulary

   You should focus on using accurate vocabulary to say exactly what you mean.

2. fix errors

   _____

3. relax and have fun

   _____

4. individual objectives

   _____

5. ask for assistance

   _____

Grammar *There is/There are*

There is and *there are* describe something that is true or exists.

Use *there is* for one thing. Use *there was* for one thing that existed in the past.

> **There is** a <u>need</u> to be very accurate in accounting. ←—— present tense
>
> **There was** a soccer <u>game</u> last night. ←—— past tense

Use *there are* for more than one thing. Use *there were* for things that existed in the past.

> **There are** many <u>restaurants</u> in my town. ←—— present tense
>
> **There were** dark <u>clouds</u> in the sky an hour ago. ←—— past tense

---

A. Complete each sentence with *there is, there was, there are,* or *there were.*

1. _____There is_____ a cat sitting on the car. I haven't seen it before.

2. _____ some sandwiches in the refrigerator a minute ago. Where are they now?

3. _____ a problem with my computer. Can you help fix it?

4. _____ a store next to the restaurant that we are going to.

5. _____ a lot of people in this restaurant yesterday.

6. _____ a bowl of nuts on the table. Please have some.

B. Correct the errors with *there is/was* and *there are/were* in the paragraph. The first error is corrected for you. There are five more.

In our kitchen, there ~~are~~ *is* a tile floor. There is pictures of my family on the

walls. There was also a table with a few chairs. Over the sink, there are a

small window. There is a closet, too. There is cabinets for dishes. There are

also the refrigerator, which is next to the stove.

C. Write sentences describing a room in your home. Use *there is/was* or *there are/were.*

1. _____

2. _____

3. _____

4. _____

5. _____

WRITING SKILL | Supporting Details

LEARN

In a personal narrative, supporting details are descriptions of feelings or events you have experienced. Details help your reader understand your problem and solution, and make your narrative more like a story. The supporting details are underlined in this short personal narrative.

New Friends

When I was a student at my university, I had a lot of friends. But when I graduated and moved to a new city, I found it hard to make new friends. *For example, I invited my coworkers to dinner, but they were always busy with family.* I felt very lonely, so I decided to join a sports club.

I play soccer every Saturday afternoon at the club. It's a lot of fun, and *a group of us go to dinner together after soccer.* Now I feel much less lonely.

APPLY

A. Discuss the questions below with a partner.

1. Read *New Friends* without the underlined sentences. How is it different?

2. How do the supporting details in *New Friends* help you understand the writer's problem and solution?

B. Read the writing model on pages 44–45 again. Underline the supporting details that describe the writer's problem and solution.

Collaborative Writing

A. Read the narrative on pages 44–45 again. With a partner, choose which sentence below best describes the writer's problem.

1. Her objective is to become an accountant, but she is more interested in sociology.

2. She wants to be a sociologist, but she thinks the job won't pay as well as being an accountant.

3. If she changes majors, she will have to stay at university for another year.

B. Work with a partner. Choose one of the other problems from activity A or use your own idea. This will become the problem in a new personal narrative. Complete the sentence below with your choice.

Problem: The writer _____, but
_____.

C. With your partner, create examples to explain the new problem. What details would help a reader understand why the problem exists?

Supporting detail: _____

Supporting detail: _____

Supporting detail: _____

D. Create a solution to the new problem. Complete the sentence below with your solution. Add examples with details that explain how the new writer made her decision.

Solution: The writer finally decided to _____.

Supporting detail: _____

Supporting detail: _____

E. Share your outline from activities C and D with the class. Discuss these questions as a class.

1. What supporting details explain the writer's problem?

2. Are there enough supporting details to understand her choice? Why, or why not?

3. Which personal narrative outline used the most interesting details?

Independent Writing

A. Think about a problem you had in your life and how you solved it. Try to think of a problem that other people may have experienced, too. Your topic may be about choosing a career, balancing time between family, friends, and work, moving to a new place, or even learning a language. Write the problem below.

Problem: _____

B. Use problem-solution organization and include supporting details. Answer the questions below as a guide.

1. How did the problem start? What events will help your reader understand the problem?

Background events: _____

_____

_____

2. When did you realize that you had a problem? How did you feel about it?

_____

_____

_____

3. What did you do to solve the problem?

_____

_____

_____

C. Include a concluding paragraph describing your life now. Fill in the sentences below to help you think of ideas.

In the end, I solved my problem by _____.

This really helped because _____.

I no longer feel _____.

Now I _____.

Now I feel _____.

D. Look at these adjectives from the model. Which adjectives describe positive feelings and which describe negative? Write them in the correct column of the chart. Add two more examples in each column.

bored	excited	new	perfect
certain	interesting	not interesting	scared

Positive feelings	Negative feelings
perfect	

VOCABULARY TIP

Use adjectives to describe your feelings throughout your story. Use a dictionary or thesaurus to help you.

E. Write your personal narrative. Use adjectives to describe your feelings and thoughts. Explain your problem and solution with supporting details from activities B and C. Remember to include the target vocabulary on page 43 in your personal narrative.

REVISE AND EDIT

A. Read your personal narrative. Answer the questions below, and make changes to your narrative as needed.

1. Check (✓) the information you included in your personal narrative.

☐ background events to understand the problem

☐ description of the problem

☐ description of the solution

☐ conclusion to describe your life now

2. Look at the information you did not include. Would adding that information make your personal narrative easier to understand?

Grammar for Editing | Subject-Verb Agreement

In English, the verb in a sentence changes based on whether the subject of the sentence is singular or plural. Add -s to the verb when the subject is a singular noun or pronoun in the third person such as *he*, *she*, or *it*.

✓ The <u>book</u> **explains** how villagers in China organize their farms. singular third-person subject

X <u>Changes</u> **happens** slowly in most societies. plural third-person subject

✓ <u>She</u> **works** today. singular third-person pronoun

X <u>I</u> **works** today. singular first-person pronoun

X <u>You</u> **works** today. singular second-person pronoun

Some nouns are always singular.

The <u>Internet</u> **changes** the way people get information and communicate.

B. Check the language in your personal narrative. Revise and edit as needed.

Language Checklist
☐ I used the target words in my personal narrative.
☐ I used adjectives to describe my feelings.
☐ I used *there is* and *there are* correctly.
☐ I added -s to verbs to agree with third-person singular subjects.

C. Check your personal narrative again. Repeat activities A and B.

Self-Assessment Review: Go back to page 43 and reassess your knowledge of the target vocabulary. How has your understanding of the words changed? What words do you feel most comfortable using now?

UNIT 5

Green Beauty

In this unit, you will

> analyze frequently asked questions (FAQs) and learn how they are used on business websites.
> use expository writing.
> increase your understanding of the target academic words for this unit.

WRITING SKILLS

> Paragraph Focus
> Giving Examples
> **GRAMMAR** Writing Questions

Self-Assessment
Think about how well you know each target word, and check (✓) the appropriate column. I have...

TARGET WORDS	never seen the word before.	heard or seen the word but am not sure what it means.	heard or seen the word and understand what it means.	used the word confidently in *either* speaking or writing.
AWL				
🔑 feature				
🔑 fee				
🔑 item				
🔑 label				
🔑 link				
🔑 partner				
🔑 previous				
🔑 purchase				

🔑 Oxford 3000™ keywords

Building Knowledge

Read these questions. Discuss your answers in a small group.

1. Do you buy things online? Why, or why not?

2. What would you want to know about a website before you shopped there for the first time?

3. Do you think natural products are healthier and safer?

Writing Models

An FAQ is a "frequently asked question, or a question customers commonly ask." Businesses often have an FAQs page on their website. This series of questions and responses answers common questions customers ask. Read an FAQ page on the website of a business that sells natural beauty products.

FAQs about Greenbeauty.com

Look beautiful, naturally

1. WHAT IS GREENBEAUTY.COM?

Greenbeauty.com is an online shop that sells only the best natural beauty products. Our soaps, shampoos, and skin-care products make you beautiful naturally. For example, our soaps

5 **feature** olive oil and coconut oil instead of rough chemicals.[1] Our site **features** only high-quality, organic products.

2. WHAT ARE ORGANIC PRODUCTS?

Organic products do not use any human-made chemicals. Each and every **item** you **purchase**
10 from our site is 100% natural. All of the ingredients come from real plants. That's good for you and good for the environment. Other beauty products are made from chemicals that can feel good but in fact are harmful.[2] For
15 instance, some chemicals other companies use can dry your skin or damage your hair! Our products contain only natural ingredients that keep you fresh and beautiful.

---

[1] *chemical:* something that has been made, sometimes by humans instead of naturally
[2] *harmful:* causing hurt or damage

3. WHAT IS THE BEST WAY TO SEARCH THIS SITE?

If you know what you want, use the search box
20 at the top of the page. Or you can use the category **links** on the left sidebar.[3] For example, if you are looking for a soap for your face, click on *Face*. Then scroll down to *soap*. Click on the **link** and find the face cleanser you want to
25 **purchase**.

All Greenbeauty.com products are organic.

4. IS GREENBEAUTY.COM ENVIRONMENTALLY FRIENDLY?

As we said **previously**, our products are chemical-free. That's good for your body but also good for the Earth. Also, all our packaging is

made of all-natural recycled materials. Even the
30 ink on our **labels** is 100% natural. Our **partners** also promise to do everything they can to protect the environment. The farmers who grow the ingredients never use chemicals, either. In addition, our factories use low-energy lights.
35 We do everything possible to protect the environment!

5. CAN I RETURN A PRODUCT IF I DON'T LIKE IT?

Of course! Returns are easy and free. First, click on the *My Order History* **link**. Then click on the word *Return* next to the image of the **item**
40 you want to return. You can then print out a free return **label**. Pack the **item** in the 100% recyclable box it came in. Finally, attach the **label** to the box and mail it to us. When we get your package, we will refund you the full price
45 of **purchase**. We even pay the shipping **fee**!

Email CustomerCare@greenbeauty.com for more information.

There is no fee for returns!

---

[3] *sidebar:* a box on a magazine page or on a website, set to the side, with information in it

LEARN

Business writing gives information quickly. Each paragraph has one topic. Answers on FAQ pages are clear and focused to help website users.

- Each answer only gives information that answers the question. The answer does not discuss other topics. All supporting details relate to the topic of the question.

- The answer often includes words and phrases from the question. The answer may define a term, give examples, or provide instructions.

- If an FAQ answer explains how to do something, such as purchase the company's products from its website, every step that the user needs to follow is included.

APPLY

A. Look at FAQ 2 on page 58 again. Check (✓) the statements below that relate to the topic of the question. Put an (**X**) next to the statements that do not relate to the question. Discuss your answers with a partner.

✓ 1. Chemicals in beauty products sometimes cause rashes.

____ 2. Organic products are often more expensive.

____ 3. Greenbeauty.com is the largest seller of organic products in the country.

____ 4. Organic products are made from naturally grown materials.

____ 5. Our organic products include herbs such as rosemary, basil, and tarragon.

B. Read FAQ 5 on page 59 again. Answer the questions below with a partner.

1. What is the first step in the process of returning an item?

_____

2. How do you get a return label?

_____

3. How should you pack the item?

_____

4. Which statement explains when you get your money back?

_____

Analyze

A. Read the FAQs on pages 58–59 again. Match the types of information often found in FAQs to the details from the writing model. There is one detail you will not use.

_d_ 1. a short description of the company

____ 2. an instruction or step to follow

____ 3. information about who the company works with

____ 4. a definition of an important term

____ 5. how to use a feature of the site

a. Organic products do not use any human-made chemicals.

b. First, click on the *My Order History* link.

c. Or you can use the category links on the left sidebar.

d. Greenbeauty.com is an online shop that sells only the best natural beauty products.

e. Returns are easy and free.

f. Our partners also promise to do everything they can to protect the environment.

B. Read the customer problems and preferences below. Work with a partner to find the Greenbeauty.com FAQ that gives the customer the information he or she needs. Write the FAQ.

1. The soap I bought smells strange. I want a refund.

   5. Can I return a product if I don't like it?

2. I want to know which categories of products are sold on Greenbeauty.com.

   _____

3. I only buy organic products.

   _____

4. I am worried that beauty products can damage my hair.

   _____

5. It is important to me that the products I buy come in recycled packaging.

   _____

C. Discuss these questions in a small group.

1. Why does a company need FAQs that are clear and easy to understand?

2. Why is it important that readers of Greenbeauty.com know what *organic* means?

3. Why do you think one FAQ discusses how environmentally friendly Greenbeauty.com is?

4. Why is it important to explain how to return products?

5. Why do you think some words such as *organic*, *natural*, and *recycled* are often repeated?

Vocabulary Activities | STEP I: Word Level

On the Internet, a *link* is "text that connects one website to another."

> *Click on this **link** to go to my website about recycling.*

The verb *link* means "to connect two things together."

> *The new highway **links** our town to the city.*

Linked is often followed by the prepositions *to* or *with*.

> *Organic farming is <u>linked to</u> protecting the environment.*

A. Complete the sentences with the correct form of the word *link*. Compare your answers with a partner. Use *to* if necessary.

1. Having a good website and selling a lot of products are strongly

   _____ *linked* _____ .

2. A website _____ companies to their customers.

3. Many people find new websites by clicking on a _____ from another website.

4. People with websites often look for other sites that are _____ the same topic.

Purchase, *label*, and *partner* can be nouns or verbs. For each word, the meanings of both forms are closely related.

Noun	Verb
You can return your **purchase** if you do not like it.	You can **purchase** a new item.
The **label** is on the bottom.	We **label** our products so you know what is in them.
My **partner** and I started a new business.	We **partner** with him because we like working together.

B. Complete the paragraph below with the correct words from the box. You will use one word twice. Write (N) if it's a noun and (V) if it's a verb.

label	partner	purchase	purchases

One way to show you care about the environment is with your

(1) ___purchases (N)___. For example, you can (2) _____ only

environmentally safe products. Some companies put a special

(3) _____ on their products to tell consumers the items are

environmentally safe. They may use a recycling symbol on their packaging,

for example. However, other companies do not (4) _____ green

products. It's important to be careful. Some companies sell products that

are good for the environment. But they (5) _____ with other

companies that hurt the environment.

C. An *item* is a single thing or object. Discuss with a partner what items each business below might sell.

> *Greenbeauty.com = organic beauty products (cleansers, shampoos, conditioners, lotions)*

1. We Love Animals
2. Kids and Crafts

3. Food for Health
4. Splish! Splash! Splosh!

Vocabulary Activities   STEP II: Sentence Level

Previous is an adjective that means "happened before something else."

> *In 2000, prices fell faster than they did in the **previous** year.*

> *I have **previous** experience working as a cashier. I did that job when I was 16.*

The adverb form is *previously*.

> *I've just written a book, but **previously** I published three articles about organic farming.*

CORPUS

D. Complete the sentences to answer the questions below. Then take turns asking and answering the questions with a partner.

1. What did you study last week?

   The previous week I studied _____ *business writing* _____.

2. Where did you study English before?

   Previously, I studied _____.

3. What was the topic of Unit 4 in this book?

   The topic of the previous unit was _____.

4. What work experience do you have?

   I previously worked _____.

5. Did you go on any trips last year?

   Yes, the previous year I went to _____.

E. A *fee* is money you pay for a service. Work with a partner. Rewrite each FAQ answer to include the type of service fee described. Use the types of fees in the box.

baggage fee	entrance fee	lab fee	membership fee	shipping fee

1. We pay the money it costs to send an item back to the store.

   We pay the shipping fee. _____

2. The money you pay for the lab covers the cost of all the tools and instruments you will use in the science-learning lab.

   _____

3. You have to pay $25 for any additional bags you take on the plane.

   _____

4. We charge $10 to enter the museum and to attend the special events happening that day.

   _____

5. It costs money to become a member of the club. This payment is charged only once.

   _____

F. Work in a small group. Imagine that your job is to design a new cell phone. Write three sentences below describing the new features. Use the word *feature* in each sentence. Use *feature* as both a noun and a verb. Share your answers with the class.

Our new cell phone will have a voice-control feature.

1. _____

2. _____

3. _____

Grammar Writing Questions

Yes/no questions begin with an auxiliary verb such as *do, be,* or *have.* The auxiliary verb comes before the subject of the sentence.

auxiliary verb   subject   main verb

Do you like movies? Yes!   present tense

Did you go to Spain last week? Yes, it was wonderful.   past tense

Will the prime minister speak today? No, not today.   future

Use *who, what, where, when, why,* or *how* to ask for specific information. These question words come before the auxiliary verb. To ask about an amount, use *how many* or *how much.* Use *how long* to ask about a length of time.

Question word   auxiliary verb   subject

When will you leave for France? Tuesday   **How long** will you be there? two weeks

What is your favorite food? rice   **How many** meals do you eat every day? three

Who called you yesterday? Clara   **Why** did she call? just to talk

A. Put the words below in the correct order to form *yes/no* questions. Take turns asking and answering the questions with a partner.

1. online / shop / you / do

   Do you shop online?

2. do / you / organic / products / buy

   _____

3. you / a / start / will / business

   _____

4. read / the / you / news / did / yesterday

   _____

B. Write an information question for each answer below. Use the question words in parentheses.

1. It is important to protect the environment. (Why)

   Why is it important to protect the environment?

2. I worked as an ecologist for six years. (How long)

   _____

3. I visited five countries last year. (How many)

   _____

4. The new laws are important because they protect the oceans from harmful chemicals. (Why)

   _____

5. I work at the United Nations. (Where)

   _____

6. I bought these for my sister Rosaria. (Who)

   _____

C. Imagine you are going to interview someone for a job at Greenbeauty.com. Write six questions to ask. Take turns asking and answering your questions with a partner.

1. *Where did you work previously?* _____

2. _____

3. _____

4. _____

5. _____

6. _____

WRITING SKILL | Giving Examples

LEARN

Use examples when writing your FAQs. Examples are supporting details that help readers create pictures in their minds. Examples make your FAQs easier to understand than an explanation alone.

- Examples should describe something that is familiar to the reader.

- Examples can be stories or experiences. However, in FAQs, examples are usually descriptions of specific things or people.

- Write examples that are easy for readers to picture in their minds.

- Use signal phrases, such as *for example* and *for instance,* to introduce examples.

Look at this FAQ from a company called Use It, Reuse It, which sells recycled products. There are two examples to explain the term *reusable items.*

10. How can I create less garbage?

The best way to make less garbage is to buy reusable items.
For example, you can buy one water bottle and use it many times. ← Example 1
One reusable bottle will keep you from throwing away many plastic
bottles. You can also reuse any jars or bottles from food that ← Example 2
you purchase. However, be sure to wash all food containers well.

APPLY

A. Read the FAQs on pages 58–59 again. Work with a partner. Find three supportive examples in the FAQs. Write them below.

Example 1: _____

_____

Example 2: _____

_____

Example 3: _____

_____

B. Discuss the questions below with your partner.

1. Read the examples you found in activity A. What information does each example help explain?

2. Read the FAQ answers without the examples you found. How are those answers different without supporting examples?

3. What signal phrases introduce examples in the FAQs?

Collaborative Writing

A. Read the description of the company Use It, Reuse It from its FAQs page below. Underline the target words from page 57 in the description.

WHAT IS USE IT, REUSE IT?

Use It, Reuse It is a new website that assists people in saving money and protecting the environment. It does this by selling products that people can use again, such as glass water bottles and cloth shopping bags. Every item we sell is made out of recycled material. In addition, every time you purchase something on our site, we donate 10% to our partner organization, Clean Air and Water.

B. Write an FAQ and answer about this website. Follow the steps below as a guide.

1. Write a question a customer might have about Use It, Reuse It.

   _____

2. Discuss your questions in a small group. As a group, choose the one you like best. Write it below:

   _____

3. How would a business answer the question? Write a clear, focused sentence to answer the question. This will be the topic sentence of your FAQ answer.

   _____

4. Give examples to help explain your answer. Use signal words and phrases to introduce your examples.

   _____

   _____

   _____

C. Share your FAQ and answer with another group. Discuss the questions below.

1. Do the examples help explain the answer?

2. Do all of the sentences in the answer connect to the topic of the question?

3. Would different examples help answer the question better? Why, or why not?

Independent Writing

A. You will write an FAQs page for a company website. You may write about a real company, or make up your own company. Brainstorm at least one question for each category in the idea map below.

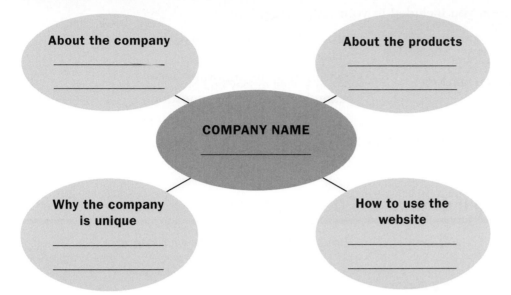

About the company
_____
_____

About the products
_____
_____

COMPANY NAME
_____

Why the company is unique
_____
_____

How to use the website
_____
_____

B. Include a description of a product or products that the website offers. Complete the sentences below as a guide.

1. Our products are unique because they are both _____ and
   (adjective)
   _____.
   (adjective)

2. Our products help you to _____ more easily.
   (verb)

3. Our products _____ better than other products.
   (verb)

4. For example, they have better _____ and _____.
   (noun)   (noun)

C. The following adjectives all describe how a product is *green*. What is the one word you want to use to describe your product? Write other adjectives with a similar meaning.

| all-natural | chemical-free | organic | recycled |

_____

D. Write your FAQs page. Include at least three questions. Use the questions you wrote in activity A and sentences you like from activity B. Include examples and adjectives. Use the target vocabulary from page 57.

> **VOCABULARY TIP**
>
> Businesses use precise language so that the answers in the FAQs provide exact information for the reader.

REVISE AND EDIT

A. Read your FAQs page. Answer the questions below, and make revisions to your page as needed.

1. Check (✓) the information you included in your FAQs page.

   ☐ information about the company

   ☐ information about products

   ☐ explanation of why the company is unique

   ☐ information on how to use the website

   ☐ definition of an important term

   ☐ examples to answer a question

2. Look at the information you did not include. Would adding that information make your FAQs page better?

Grammar for Editing   Indefinite and Definite Articles

Use the indefinite articles *a* and *an* to write about a general example or category of something.

> He is <u>a</u> teacher and his wife is <u>a</u> doctor.

> I want to buy <u>an</u> electric toothbrush, but I don't know what kind is best.

Do not use the articles *a* and *an* with plural nouns or with non-count nouns.

> They are teachers.

> I prefer toothpaste with a mint flavor.

Use the definite article *the* to refer to a specific thing.

> <u>The</u> English teacher told us we have a quiz tomorrow.

> <u>The</u> website I looked at yesterday sold a lot of toothbrushes.

B. Check the language on your FAQs page. Revise and edit as needed.

Language Checklist
☐ I used target words on my FAQs page.
☐ I used adjectives to describe my product precisely.
☐ I formed questions correctly.
☐ I used indefinite and definite articles correctly.

C. Check your FAQs page again. Repeat activities A and B.

Self-Assessment Review: Go back to page 57 and reassess your knowledge of the target vocabulary. How has your understanding of the words changed? What words do you feel most comfortable using now?

UNIT 6

Ice Sheets in Mongolia

In this unit, you will

> see how an analysis is used to discuss issues in science.
> use factual explanations.
> increase your understanding of the target academic words for this unit.

WRITING SKILLS

> Introductions
> Cohesion
> **GRAMMAR** Conjunctions and Transitions

Self-Assessment

Think about how well you know each target word, and check (✓) the appropriate column. I have...

TARGET WORDS	never seen the word before.	heard or seen the word but am not sure what it means.	heard or seen the word and understand what it means.	used the word confidently in *either* speaking or writing.
AWL				
🔑 access				
🔑 area				
🔑 define				
🔑 illustrate				
🔑 issue				
🔑 plus				
🔑 task				
🔑 temporary				

🔑 Oxford 3000™ keywords

Building Knowledge

Read these questions. Discuss your answers in a small group.

1. Do you enjoy reading about science? Why, or why not?

2. What do you know about the theory of global warming?

3. How are people trying to stop global warming?

Writing Model

An analysis describes a project in science and then points out its advantages and disadvantages. Read this analysis of the Mongolian Ice Sheets Project.

The Mongolian Ice Sheets Project

THE PROJECT

The Mongolian Ice Sheets Project is a bold plan to cool Ulan Bator in summer and to slow global warming. Ulan Bator, the capital of Mongolia, is located in an **area** of Asia that gets cold in
5 winter and very hot in summer. Temperatures can reach 38°C (100°F). These temperatures are dangerous. Global warming makes the problem more serious. So, scientists plan to create *naled*s on the Tuul River near the city. Naleds are
10 **defined** as "ice that is made of many layers.[1]" They will not melt until summer. Therefore, cold air from the ice will keep the city cooler.

Mongolia in summer

Naleds form naturally on frozen rivers in winter. Water comes up through cracks in the ice. Then
15 that water freezes on top in a new layer. This can happen many times, forming many layers of ice on a river. Similarly, the human-made naleds will have many layers. However, they will be thicker.

They will last longer than natural ice. The **task**
20 of making thicker layers is not difficult. First, engineers drill holes in the ice to **access** unfrozen water below. Next, they pump water through the holes onto the top of the ice. Then the water freezes in a new layer on top. Finally,

---

[1] *layer:* something flat that lies on another thing

25 the engineers repeat the process in order to build up the ice. In the end, there will be thick ice that will last for a long time.

ADVANTAGES AND DISADVANTAGES

There are many advantages to this project. It uses a natural solution that does not pollute the
30 environment. This is a big **plus** that keeps costs down. Naleds can also be a long-lasting, not **temporary**, solution. Finally, building the naleds means jobs every winter.

However, there are also disadvantages. It is
35 still very expensive to pay for the personnel[2] and machines needed to build the naleds. Also, some people believe that the cooled air will stay in the **area** by the river, and not spread[3] across the city. Finally, many people don't believe
40 naleds will be a long-term[4] solution to global warming. They believe human-made naleds may cool one city, but not help fix the worldwide problem.

CONCLUSION

In my opinion, the way the project uses nature
45 **plus** the chances of success are worth the

Mongolia in winter

large costs. Other projects could be more expensive or harder to complete. This project will be less damaging to the environment. In fact, it **illustrates** how a natural resource
50 helps resolve a serious **issue**. Other cities with **access** to water could copy this idea. I believe scientists, engineers, and the people of Ulan Bator should move forward and start this project.

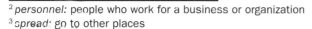

[2] *personnel:* people who work for a business or organization
[3] *spread:* go to other places
[4] *long-term:* for a long period of time

LEARN

An introduction tells the reader the topic of your analysis. It also provides important background information. After reading the introduction, readers will know what project the analysis is about. Consider these steps when you write an introduction of a project analysis.

1. Write a sentence that introduces the topic, or main idea, of the analysis. It should explain what the project is.

   The Karakum Canal Dam will create a water reservoir for people who live in the Karakum Desert.

2. Describe the setting, or where the project takes place. Include not only important information about the place, but also the reasons for the project.

   The Karakum Desert in Turkmenistan has very little water. However, the people who live there need drinking water.

3. Describe how the project will solve the problem or issue.

   The dam will provide drinking water for people in the desert.

4. Explain important information or key terms for the reader.

   A dam is a large barrier that blocks rivers in order to create artificial lakes.

5. You may or may not include your opinion about the topic in the introduction.

   This project has a good chance of success.

APPLY

A. Read the first paragraph of the analysis on page 72 again. Answer the questions below in a small group. Note the line where you find the answer.

1. What is the name of the project? Which sentence clearly states what this project aims to do?

   _____

2. In what city will the project take place? Where is that city?

   _____

3. What problem will the project try to solve?

   _____

4. What key term does the author explain? How is this term related to the project?

   _____

5. Reread the first sentence. What does the word *bold* mean? From this word, what do you think the author's opinion of the project is?

   _____

B. Underline sentences in the introduction that tell you about the problem. Write the problem in your own words.

1. *Ulan Bator is very hot in summer.*

2. _____

3. _____

Analyze

A. Read the project analysis on pages 72–73 again. Put the steps of the project in order. Then write the signal words that help you understand the order.

Activity	Order	Signal words
Water is pumped up over the top of the ice.		
The thick ice will last longer in summer and cool the city.		
The process is repeated to build thick ice.		
The water freezes in a new layer.		
Holes are drilled through layers of ice in winter.	*1*	*First*

B. Underline the sentences in the project analysis on pages 72–73 that give each advantage and disadvantage of the project. Write the keywords for each sentence.

Advantages

1. *natural solution – does not pollute environment*

2. _____

3. _____

4. _____

Disadvantages

1. _____

2. _____

3. _____

C. Read the last paragraph of the project analysis on page 73. Discuss the following questions in a small group.

1. Conclusions may summarize the main idea, ask readers to do something, or give the author's opinion. How does this analysis conclude?

2. What keywords in the conclusion helped you understand its purpose?

3. What reasons does the author give for this opinion? Is this information found anywhere else in the analysis?

4. How would the conclusion be different if the author only summarized the project?

Vocabulary Activities STEP I: Word Level

Area can mean "a part of a place such as a city or country or even the world."

> I like this **area** of the city. The buildings are very beautiful.

Area can also mean "a space used for a specific purpose."

> The quiet **area** of the library is where people read or study in silence.

In mathematics, the *area* refers to "the amount of space covered by a flat surface or shape."

> The **area** of this room is 12 square meters.

 CORPUS

A. Work with a partner. Match the first part of each sentence with the correct ending to make a definition. There is one extra ending.

_a_ 1. The area of a shape is
___ 2. A waiting area is
___ 3. The coastal area is
___ 4. The area of the kitchen is
___ 5. The industrial area is

a. how big it is.
b. a place where people sleep.
c. the part of town with lots of factories.
d. where you wait for a doctor.
e. the part of a place near the ocean.
f. the size of the room.

B. Work with a partner. Match each person with what he or she needs access to in order to complete his or her daily tasks.

_c_ 1. a photographer
___ 2. a student
___ 3. a truck driver
___ 4. a doctor
___ 5. a construction worker

a. roads and highways
b. building materials
c. a camera and picture-editing software
d. medicines and exam tools
e. textbooks and the Internet

C. Read the paragraph. Then answer the questions using the words in parentheses.

Access to clean water is a big problem. The Clean Machine will fix this problem. It will make any water clean enough to drink. It will also make water clean for bathing. It comes with a filter. You need to change the filter every month. It does not work forever.

1. What problem is this machine going to solve? (issue)

_____

2. What job will it do? (task)

_____

3. What other thing can it do? (plus)

_____

4. What part of the machine needs to be changed? (temporary)

_____

The verb *define* means "to tell exactly what a word means." *Define* often appears with the preposition *as*.

> A banana is **defined** as a long yellow fruit.

The noun form is *definition*.

> The **definition** of a table is "a piece of furniture with legs and a flat top."

CORPUS

D. Work with a partner. Write your own definition of each word below. Write complete sentences using the words *define* or *definition*.

1. honesty

   The definition of honesty is "always telling the truth."

2. success

   _____

3. friend

   _____

4. fun

   _____

The verb *illustrate* means "to use examples or pictures to make the meaning of something clearer."

*He **illustrated** his talk with stories about his life.*

An *illustration* is "an example or picture that explains something." It can refer to a story, drawing, or diagram.

*He described the happiest day of his life as an **illustration** of what happiness means.*

*This book has beautiful **illustrations** of the important events in the story.*

E. Complete the sentences below with words from activity D and the correct form of *illustrate*.

1. A child who tells his parents he did something bad ___illustrates___ the word ___honesty___.

2. A person who always helps you is an _____ of the word _____.

3. Getting a good job _____ the idea of _____.

4. One _____ of _____ is going to the beach with family or friends.

5. A nice flower _____ what many people think of as _____.

F. What are the tasks that you do regularly? Is there a task you do every day, about once per week, about once per month, and about once per year? Write examples of your regular tasks below. Use a form of the word *task* in your answer.

1. Daily task:

   One of my daily tasks is packing my bag for class.

   _____

2. Weekly task:

   _____

3. Monthly task:

   _____

4. Yearly task:

   _____

Grammar | Conjunctions and Transitions

Some conjunctions connect two parts of a sentence. *And, or,* and *but* are common conjunctions used between two ideas in the same sentence.

Use *and* to connect similar ideas or information.

> The Mongolian Ice Sheets Project is a bold plan to cool Ulan Bator in summer _and_ slow global warming.

Use *or* to show choice.

> Other projects could be more expensive _or_ harm the environment.

Use *but* to show that two things are different, or that they contrast.

> They believe human-made naleds may cool one city, _but_ not fix the worldwide problem.

Transition words such as *similarly* and *however* connect the ideas of two sentences. The word *similarly* shows comparison. The word *however* shows contrast. These words usually go at the beginning of a sentence.

> Naleds form naturally on frozen rivers in winter. _Similarly_, the human-made naleds will have many layers. _However_, they will be thicker.

A. Complete the paragraph below with the correct conjunctions and transitions. Compare your answers with a partner.

Projects like dams and mines can provide energy _____ make

an area easier for people to live in. _____, there could be

disadvantages. Until a project is finished, no one knows if it will solve a

problem _____ just cause more problems. Some people feel that

scientists and engineers should not build large projects that change nature,

_____ others feel that big projects are a good way to improve

people's lives. _____, people have different opinions on how

effective any particular project will be.

B. Work with a partner. Combine each pair of sentences using the conjunction in parentheses.

1. The project will be expensive. The project will be difficult. (and)

   The project will be expensive and difficult.

2. I think this project has advantages. It also has some disadvantages. (but)

   _____

3. Building a dam will solve the problem. Changing the direction of the river will solve the problem. (or)

   _____

4. The new computer has a fast processor. It works well. (and)

   _____

C. Finish the sentences below in a small group. Use your own ideas.

1. I did my homework, but _____*I forgot to bring it to school*_____.

2. After school, we can go home or _____.

3. My friend did not feel well this morning, but _____.

4. _____, but I will stay at home.

5. I enjoy _____ and

   _____.

D. Work with a partner. Discuss three things you both do or like. Discuss three things that only one of you does or likes. Write sentences using *however* and *similarly* to tell about your similarities and differences.

   I like to watch soccer. Similarly, Ali likes to watch soccer.
   I drink coffee in the morning. However, Ali drinks coffee in the evening.

Similarities

1. _____

2. _____

3. _____

Differences

1. _____

2. _____

3. _____

WRITING SKILL · Cohesion

LEARN

Cohesion means "connecting ideas and information." In cohesive writing, the relationships between ideas and sentences are clear. Each sentence should relate to the idea, or sentence, before it. Each paragraph should also be connected to information in an earlier paragraph. Follow these steps to write cohesively:

- Outline each paragraph so that each sentence relates to its main idea.

- Use transition words.

to give an example	*for example, such as, for instance*
to give a reason	*since, because*
to add new information	*also, in addition*
to compare	*however, similarly*
to give a suggestion	*I think, it would be good, in my opinion*

- Start each paragraph with a sentence that connects to an earlier paragraph.

- When you edit your writing, make sure all the sentences relate to the main idea. Delete sentences that are not connected to the main idea.

APPLY

With a partner, read the description of a problem and solution. Answer the questions.

> The project to build a park will be expensive. It will be a beautiful park, though. First of all, the cost of the materials will be one million dollars. And the cost of hiring workers may be even higher.
>
> This is too expensive for our city. The city just built an expensive library. In my opinion, we should not build a flower garden in the park. This will make the project affordable because it will reduce the cost by 30 percent. People will still enjoy the new park without the expensive garden.

1. Cross out a sentence in each paragraph that you would delete for cohesion.

2. How do the sentences in the first paragraph connect to the main idea? Do they give examples, suggestions, or comparisons?

3. How does the first sentence in the second paragraph connect to the first paragraph?

4. Which sentence in the second paragraph suggests a solution?

5. How does the last sentence connect to the suggestion? Does it give another comparison, suggestion, or reason?

Collaborative Writing

A. Read the project analysis on pages 72–73 again. The sentences below each connect to a main idea in the analysis. In a small group, discuss the best place in the text to put each sentence.

1. Naleds can grow to seven meters thick.

2. Engineers need to find a location where cooled air moves towards the city.

3. The thicker layers of ice may hurt wildlife and the river environment.

4. Winds may blow the cool air away from the city.

5. Temperatures in winter are as low as -30°F (-33°C).

6. The project will make Mongolia famous as a country of innovation.

B. Pick at least two details from activity A. How are those details related to the ideas already in the analysis? Write sentences below using transition words to signal the relationship between ideas. Underline the transitions you use.

The project will make Mongolia famous as a country of innovation, <u>and</u> other

countries with access to water could copy this idea.

_____

_____

_____

C. Rewrite the paragraphs of the analysis where your group decides to add the new details. Use transition words for cohesion.

D. Share your rewritten analysis with another group. Discuss the questions below.

1. Why did your group choose the new details you included? Did another group choose different details? Why?

2. Are the new details related to the main topic of the paragraph where your group placed them?

3. What changes did you make for cohesion?

4. How did including these details change the project analysis?

Independent Writing

A. You will write an analysis of a solar power project. Read notes about the project below.

Location: desert in the southwestern United States

Problem: population is growing, needs access to more power

Purpose: use natural resources of desert, create more electricity

Project: build a solar power station in the desert

Key term: *solar power* means "energy from the sun"

B. Read the statements about the project. Write *A* if it is an advantage or *D* if it is a disadvantage. Do you know anything about solar panels or solar power stations? Add your own ideas.

_____ 1. Solar power creates little pollution.

_____ 2. Desert sand can cover the solar panels.

_____ 3. Water is needed to cool the station, but there is little water in the desert.

_____ 4. Solar panels last a long time and require little repair.

_____ 5. Solar panels are _____ to build.

_____ 6. There is plenty of _____ in the desert.

_____ 7. _____

_____ 8. _____

C. Include your opinion in your analysis. Answer the questions below to help form your opinion.

1. Where will it be located? _____

2. What problem will it help solve? _____

3. What are the most important advantages and disadvantages?

_____

_____

4. Do you think this is a good project? Why?

_____

VOCABULARY TIP

Comparative adjectives can be useful to show opinions. Comparative adjectives are formed by adding *-er* at the end of an adjective or by putting the word *more* or *less* before the adjective.

D. In the writing model, find the comparative form of the adjectives listed below. Only two of the adjectives form the comparative with the word *more* or *less*. Circle those two adjectives.

cool	expensive	hard	long	serious	thick

E. Outline an analysis. Write key words in the following chart to organize your ideas cohesively in each paragraph.

Introduction	Analysis	Opinion
Main idea: _____	Main idea: _____	Main idea: _____
1. _____	1. _____	1. _____
2. _____	2. _____	2. _____
3. _____	3. _____	3. _____

F. Write an analysis of the solar station project. Describe the advantages and disadvantages. Give your opinion of the project. Use conjunctions, transitions, adjectives, and the target words on page 71.

A. Read your analysis. Answer the questions below, and make revisions to your analysis as needed.

1. Check (✓) the information you included in your analysis.

   ☐ description of the project   ☐ description of the problem

   ☐ description of the setting of   ☐ advantages
   the project

                                       ☐ disadvantages

   ☐ definitions of important terms   ☐ concluding opinion

2. Look at the information you did not include. Would adding that information make your analysis more informative or complete?

Grammar for Editing   Commas

If two ideas in a sentence both have a subject and a verb, and the ideas are connected by a conjunction, separate them with a comma. Place the comma before the conjunction.

> **Spain's football team won the World Cup, and Mexico's team won the gold medal in the Olympics.**

Commas also separate items in a list of three or more things.

> **The flag is red, white, and blue.**

B. Check the language in your analysis. Revise and edit as needed.

Language Checklist
☐ I used target words in my analysis.
☐ I used transition words and conjunctions.
☐ I used comparative adjectives correctly in my analysis.
☐ I used commas correctly.

C. Check your analysis again. Repeat activities A and B.

Self-Assessment Review: Go back to page 71 and reassess your knowledge of the target vocabulary. How has your understanding of the words changed? What words do you feel most comfortable using now?

UNIT

7

When the Earth Moves

In this unit, you will

> analyze summaries and learn how they are used to explain scientific research.
> use extended definition writing.
> increase your understanding of the target academic words for this unit.

WRITING SKILLS

> Definitions
> Summarizing
> **GRAMMAR** Modal Verbs *Can*, *May*, *Should*, and *Must*

Self-Assessment

Think about how well you know each target word, and check (✓) the appropriate column. I have…

TARGET WORDS	never seen the word before.	heard or seen the word but am not sure what it means.	heard or seen the word and understand what it means.	used the word confidently in *either* speaking or writing.
AWL				
🔑 acknowledge				
🔑 attach				
🔑 code				
🔑 couple				
🔑 device				
🔑 highlight				
🔑 role				
🔑 topic				

🔑 Oxford 3000™ keywords

Building Knowledge

Read these questions. Discuss your answers in a small group.

1. Have you ever experienced an earthquake?

2. How can people prepare for earthquakes?

3. Do you think it is possible to predict earthquakes?

Writing Model

A summary includes only the most important information on a topic. Read about an earth science project. Then read the summary.

Ozone Gas and Predicting Earthquakes

The subject, or **topic**, of our project is the **role** ozone gas may play in predicting earthquakes. Ozone gas is a natural gas. It is found in Earth's atmosphere.[1] Recent research at the University
5 of Virginia shows that ozone gas may appear when rocks break apart. This is exciting new research. This tells us that ozone gas may help us know when an earthquake is going to happen.

10   To understand this, we need to understand how earthquakes happen. The top layer of Earth is called the *crust*. The crust "floats" above the inner layer of the earth similar to ice floating on a river. It is divided into 12 plates, or enormous
15 sections of Earth. The edges of these plates are called *fault lines*. These plates are not **attached** to each other. In fact, they move slowly, at only a **couple** of centimeters a year. The moving plates rub against each other. Parts of them can stick[2] to each other. While the edges of the plates are stuck to each other, other parts of each plate are still moving. The plates pull at the
20 stuck edges. This creates a lot of pressure.[3] The pressure continues to build until the edges of the plates separate. This forces the plates to move

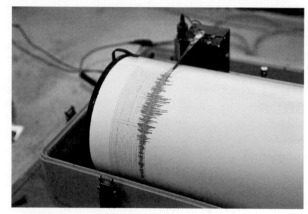

Scientists can measure earthquakes. The next step is to predict them.

---

[1] *atmosphere:* the air that surrounds Earth
[2] *stick:* to fix in one place; to not be able to move
[3] *pressure:* the force, or power, that presses on something

suddenly at the fault lines. We experience this as the ground shaking, or as an earthquake.

I want to **highlight** that before the plates move, the pressure breaks up underground rock. Studies show that breaking rocks can release, or send out, ozone gas. Therefore, my team will place **devices** that measure levels of ozone gas near fault lines. If my theory[4] is correct, ozone gas levels in the air should increase just before an earthquake.

I **acknowledge** that more experiments must be done to prove this theory. We need to be sure the rising ozone gas comes only from underground rocks breaking apart. However, if this is true, my research can help predict earthquakes. Scientists may be able to **code** maps with ozone gas levels. This would help us know the chances of an earthquake happening. It is our hope that this research will help protect people from earthquakes.

---

[4] *theory:* an idea that explains how or why something happens

Summary

The **topic** of the research is ozone gas and how it may help in predicting earthquakes. Ozone is a natural gas. Ozone gas may be released when rocks break before an earthquake. Earthquakes are caused by plates moving against each other at fault lines, or the edges of plates. Plates are large pieces of ground that move very slowly over time. The surface of Earth is made up of 12 plates. The plates rub against each other. Sometimes two pieces get **attached**, which creates pressure. This causes a **couple** of things to happen. First, it can break underground rocks. Second, it will lead to an earthquake. Ozone gas may be released by the breaking rocks. Measuring the ozone gas rising from underground could predict an earthquake. The theory is not proven yet. To test it, the research team will measure ozone gas near fault lines with special **devices**. To prove this theory, the ozone gas levels must rise just before an earthquake.

LEARN

A scientific text often uses complicated words or terms. Summaries of these texts include definitions of key terms.

Follow these steps to use definitions in a summary:

1. Identify the key terms. These can be important words or ideas.

2. Use simple language to explain what the terms mean or how they work. Refer to things that the reader may already know about. Use easier synonyms for words.

3. Explain how each term is related to the larger topic and to other important terms.

Definitions can be part of a sentence, or they can be in a sentence alone:

Writing Definitions	
Use a comma to separate a synonym or short description in the same sentence.	Earthquakes can be *devastating*, or **very harmful.**
Provide a short description in a separate sentence.	An *epicenter* **is the point directly above the place where fault lines move and cause an earthquake.**
Write several sentences to define a complicated term.	An *aftershock* **is a smaller earthquake that happens after the main earthquake. After fault lines move, the plates have to settle into place. Sometimes they move enough to create a small earthquake.**

APPLY

A. Read the project report and summary on pages 86–87 again. Work with a partner. Underline details in the writing model that define each term in the left column below. Then match the term with its definition in the right column.

a. topic

b. the crust

c. plates

d. fault lines

e. ozone gas

f. earthquake

_a_ 1. the subject of the text or project

____ 2. ground shakes because pressure causes fault lines to move

____ 3. the top layer of Earth

____ 4. large moving sections of Earth that sometimes stick together

____ 5. where two plates meet

____ 6. a gas found naturally in the air

B. With a partner, answer the questions about the definitions used in the writing model on pages 86–87.

1. Which term in the first paragraph of the project report is defined with a synonym in the same sentence?

   _____

2. In the first paragraph, one term is defined in two sentences. Which term is it?

   _____

3. What is the definition of *fault lines* in the summary? How is this different from the way the writer defines the term in the project report?

   _____

   _____

4. Which definition in the project report compares a key term to something that readers are already familiar with?

   _____

Analyze

A. Read the project report on pages 86–87 again. Work with a partner. Match each paragraph with its purpose in the box below. Write keywords to support your answers.

> a. introduces the subject and purpose of the project
> b. explains what will be tested and how
> c. explains how the project may be useful
> d. gives important background information about earthquakes

_a_ 1. Paragraph 1

Keywords: *the topic of our project* _____

____ 2. Paragraph 2

Keywords: _____

____ 3. Paragraph 3

Keywords: _____

____ 4. Paragraph 4

Keywords: _____

B. Match the purposes from activity A with the sentences from the summary on page 87.

_d_ 1. Earthquakes are caused by plates moving against each other at fault lines, or the edges of plates. Plates are large pieces of ground that move very slowly over time.

___ 2. To test it, the research team will measure ozone gas near fault lines with special devices. To prove this theory, the ozone gas levels must rise just before an earthquake.

___ 3. The topic of the research is ozone gas and how it may help in predicting earthquakes.

___ 4. Measuring the ozone gas rising from underground could predict an earthquake.

C. Discuss these questions about the summary on page 87 in a small group.

1. Why do you think the writer defined *ozone gas*, but not *earthquake*?

2. How is the definition of *plates* important to the larger topic of earthquakes?

3. Why is explaining *pressure* important when writing about the theory for predicting earthquakes?

4. Who do you think is the intended audience—scientists or the general public? How does the writer's explanation of how an earthquake happens indicate the intended audience?

5. How does the writer make it clear that this topic is about an unproven theory, not a fact?

Vocabulary Activities STEP I: Word Level

To *attach* means "to connect one thing to another thing."

*I **attached** the stamp to the letter before mailing it.*

The noun *attachment* can refer to "a document or file connected to an email."

*I got your email and the **attachments**. I will sign the forms today.*

The adjective form is *attached*. It can also refer to "liking someone or something very much."

*We've lived here for years and are very **attached** to this house.*

CORPUS

A. Work with a partner. Fill in sentences with the correct form of *attach*.

1. When you apply for a job, don't forget to _____*attach*_____ your résumé.

2. I felt _____ to my school and was almost sad to graduate.

3. The professor asked us to send our essays as an _____ to an email.

4. I _____ my keys to my bag so I would not lose them.

A *code* is "a way of giving information with letters, numbers, or special signs."

The bar **code** on the box of cereal tells a computer how much it costs.

A ZIP **code** is a group of numbers that tell where your letter should go.

A *code* is often used to write secret messages.

A simple **code** is to write 1 for the letter A, 2 for the letter B, and so on.

CORPUS

B. Work with a partner. Use the words in the box to name what type of code the statements below describe.

country	Morse	postal	security

1. To enter our house, you have to press a series of numbers called a
   security code. Otherwise, an alarm goes off.

2. Dots and dashes or short and long noises are used in _____.

3. Numbers or letters that are part of an address on a letter are called a
   _____.

4. The sequence of numbers you dial on the phone to call someone in
   another country is the _____.

C. Complete the paragraph with the correct form of the words in the box.

acknowledge	couple	highlight	role	topic

Thank you for coming to tonight's talk. The (1) _____ of the

lecture is unusual events before earthquakes. There are a (2) _____

of things that often happen before earthquakes. First, some people believe

that animals start acting strangely before earthquakes. Another event

(3) _____ an interesting theory. Earthquakes usually happen at

high tide. So tides may play a (4) _____ in earthquakes. Maybe in

the future these events will help us predict earthquakes. However, I must

(5) _____ that right now it is impossible.

D. Work with a partner. Read each task below. Complete the chart by writing the device that would help a person do each task.

Task	Device
clean clothing	*washing machine*
talk to someone far away	
cook food	
clean floors	
watch a movie at home	

Vocabulary Activities STEP II: Sentence Level

To *acknowledge* something is "to state or agree that it is true." Often it is something that is not good.

> I **acknowledge** my error. I hope that you will forgive me.

To *acknowledge* can mean "to show you have noticed someone or something."

> He **acknowledged** his friend by waving.

To *acknowledge* can also mean "to show you received something from someone, especially to show you are thankful for receiving something."

> He sent me a letter to **acknowledge** my gift.

CORPUS

E. Work with a partner. Change the phrases below to use the correct form of the word *acknowledge*. Then complete the sentences with your own details.

1. The soccer player admitted...

   The soccer player acknowledged that he did not play well that day.

2. His email thanked us for...

   _____

3. It is always important to show...

   _____

4. I waved to my friend when...

   _____

5. The company explained its mistake...

   _____

To *highlight* something means "to show that it is important so that people notice it."

*My essay **highlights** the role of Leonardo da Vinci in inventing the airplane.*

*His speech **highlighted** the need to predict earthquakes better.*

CORPUS

F. Read the report titles below. Match each title with the natural disaster that would be described in the report. Then write sentences describing what problem the report highlights. There is one extra natural disaster.

<u>a</u> 1. *Buildings That Can Survive Shaking*

     2. *Storing Water for Dry Times*

     3. *When Rivers Overflow and Harm Farmland*

     4. *Stopping Lava Flows*

     5. *Heavy Winds Can Damage Ships*

a. earthquakes

b. volcano

c. landslide

d. hurricane

e. flood

f. drought

1. *This report highlights the fact that earthquakes shake buildings.*

2. _____

3. _____

4. _____

5. _____

Grammar Modal Verbs *Can, May, Should,* and *Must*

Modal verbs include *can, may, should,* and *must.* A modal comes before the base form of a verb. Never add an *-s* to the ending of the modal verb or to the base form verb.

She can speak three languages.
   modal   base form

He should win the game.
   modal   base form

Modal verbs like *should* and *may* show how sure you are that something happened, is happening, or will happen.

Ozone gas *may* appear when rocks break apart. ⟵ less sure

Ozone gas levels *should* increase just before an earthquake. ⟵ more sure

The modal verb *can* shows that you know something is possible because it has happened before.

Parts of them *can* stick to each other.

The modal verbs *should* and *must* tell if something is necessary or not.

More experiments *must* be done to prove this theory.

A. Replace the underlined words with *may, can, should,* or *must.* It is possible that more than one modal verb is correct. Discuss your answers with a partner.

1. High tides <u>are able to</u> damage the beach. _____

2. We <u>have to</u> correct the mistake in the data. _____

3. Volcano eruptions <u>possibly</u> have positive effects on the environment.

_____

4. An eclipse of the sun <u>is likely to</u> happen tomorrow at 3 p.m. _____

B. Read the instructions about how to stay safe during an earthquake. Complete each sentence with a modal verb. There is more than one correct answer.

First of all, an earthquake (1) _____ happen at any time. You

(2) _____ always be prepared. If you are inside, stand in a

doorway. It is possible that you (3) _____ be outside, too. In that

case, you (4) _____ stand far from buildings and trees. If you are

hurt, you (5) _____ go to the hospital. This is very important.

C. Make five predictions about what will happen tomorrow. Use modal verbs to show how sure you are. Write about your classes, what you will eat, people you will meet, or any other activity.

Tomorrow we may study the past tense in English. _____

1. _____

2. _____

3. _____

4. _____

5. _____

WRITING SKILL · Summarizing

LEARN

When you summarize a difficult topic, focus on only the most important information.

- Give only the main idea and key supporting details.

- Do not copy words or sentences from the text that you are summarizing. Use synonyms and other words that are your own.

- Do not include your opinions.

APPLY

Read the project report and summary on pages 86–87 again. How does the writer summarize the main idea and details of the first paragraph? Answer these questions with a partner.

1. What sentence in the summary tells the main idea of the first paragraph of the report?

2. What words does the summary writer use in place of the word *role* from the original project report?

3. Which supporting detail in the summary is a definition?

4. What details from the project report are not included in the summary?

Collaborative Writing

A. In a small group, read the passage *The Power of Earthquakes*. Underline the target words from page 85.

> *The Power of Earthquakes*
>
> Earthquakes have interesting causes. The Earth's crust is divided into huge plates. The plates move very slowly. Fault lines are where the plates meet. There are several well-known locations of fault lines, such as the ones near and under Tokyo, Japan. The edges of plates are rough, so fault lines sometimes stick together. But the plates keep moving. The stuck edges of the plates pull against each other. This causes energy to build up in the form of pressure. Eventually, the pressure becomes too strong and the fault lines slip or shift. The earth breaks! This releases energy that causes an earthquake.
>
> A seismograph is a device that measures the strength of earthquakes. It measures how much the ground shakes during an earthquake. The simplest kind of

seismograph has a base. There is also a hanging weight called a pendulum attached to a pen or writing device. Because the pendulum hangs, it does not move during an earthquake. But the base does. The pen makes a mark on a piece of paper on the base. This shows how far the base moved relative to the pendulum. Seismographs are computerized these days, but the way they work has not changed very much. An earthquake in Chile in 1960 is the most powerful ever measured by a seismograph.

Another way to measure an earthquake is by the amount of destruction, or damage, it causes. When earthquakes shake the earth, they can cause a lot of damage. Buildings and trees may fall in a powerful earthquake. Earthquakes can also cause the ground to rupture, or open up. In movies, we sometimes see the earth opening up during an earthquake. This can really happen! Finally, even if an earthquake happens far from cities or buildings, it can cause tsunamis, or waves, as high as 100 feet (32 meters). Tsunamis can do a lot of damage very quickly. When we say an earthquake is powerful, we sometimes mean it does a lot of damage!

B. Work with a partner. Take notes on three main ideas and the key details in *The Power of Earthquakes*. Also list details that you will not include in a summary, such as opinions and less important information.

Main ideas and key details	Less important information
Plates moving against each other at fault lines cause earthquakes.	

C. Share your chart with the class. You may cross out details that you no longer think are important or you may add details that your classmates have included.

Independent Writing

A. You will write a summary of *The Power of Earthquakes*. In your own words, write the three main ideas from your chart in activity B of Collaborative Writing.

1. Main idea: _____

_____

2. Main idea: _____

_____

3. Main idea: _____

_____

B. Include an explanation of a seismograph in your own words. Match the phrases that have the same meaning.

____ 1. the strength of an earthquake   a. movement of the foundation

____ 2. the ground shakes   b. the size of an earthquake

____ 3. during an earthquake   c. when an earthquake happens

____ 4. how far the base moved   d. comparing it to

____ 5. relative to   e. the ground moves

VOCABULARY TIP

The writer of *The Power of Earthquakes* uses vocabulary to explain concepts, or ideas, in earth science. This vocabulary will help you to support the main ideas in your summary.

C. Complete the sentences below using the words in the box. Then circle the words you will use in your summary.

energy	measure	pressure	release	ruptures

1. _____ builds when one thing presses on another.

2. To _____ something means to let it go.

3. _____ is the power to do something. For example, electrical

   _____ powers the lights in your house.

4. To _____ something is to find out the size or amount of something.

5. Something _____ when it breaks open or into pieces.

D. Write your summary in a paragraph. Use your outline from activity A to organize your ideas. Include only the most important ideas. Define the important terms and describe information in your own words. Use words that are related to earth science and the target words on page 85.

A. Read your summary. Answer the questions below, and make revisions to your summary as needed.

1. Check (✓) the information you included in your summary.

   ☐ main ideas

   ☐ synonyms for words from text

   ☐ definitions of key terms

   ☐ key details in my own words

2. Look at the information you did not include. Would adding that information make your summary better?

Grammar for Editing | Base Form of the Verb

Modal verbs are always followed by the base form of the verb.

> ✓ He _can_ speak English.

> ✗ I _can_ speaks English.

> ✓ We _may_ go to the movies later if you want to join us.

> ✗ We _may_ to go to the movies later if you want to join us.

> ✓ It's very late. She _must_ be home now.

> ✗ It's very late. She _must_ is home now.

B. Check the language in your summary. Revise and edit as needed.

Language Checklist
☐ I used target words in my summary.
☐ I used words and terms related to earth science.
☐ I used modal verbs to show certainty and necessity.
☐ I used the base form of verbs following a modal verb.

C. Check your summary again. Repeat activities A and B.

Self-Assessment Review: Go back to page 85 and reassess your knowledge of the target vocabulary. How has your understanding of the words changed? What words do you feel most comfortable using now?

UNIT
8

Eating Right

In this unit, you will

> analyze how a script is written for public service announcements (PSAs).
> use cause-and-effect writing.
> increase your understanding of the target academic words for this unit.

WRITING SKILLS

> Cause and Effect
> Hooks
> **GRAMMAR** *This* and *That*

Self-Assessment

Think about how well you know each target word, and check (✓) the appropriate column. I have…

TARGET WORDS	never seen the word before.	heard or seen the word but am not sure what it means.	heard or seen the word and understand what it means.	used the word confidently in *either* speaking or writing.
AWL				
🔑 adult				
🔑 appreciate				
🔑 available				
🔑 chart				
🔑 intelligence				
🔑 lecture				
🔑 minor				
🔑 remove				

🔑 Oxford 3000™ keywords

Building Knowledge

Read these questions. Discuss your answers in a small group.

1. Do you eat healthy food most of the time?

2. Why do people eat food that they know is bad for them?

3. Where do you get information about food and nutrition?

Writing Models

A public service announcement, or PSA, is a short announcement made to give people helpful information. A PSA is read out loud on the radio or performed on television. Read the PSAs about healthy food.

Breakfast: Not a Minor Meal

Did you have breakfast today? Breakfast is the most important meal of the day. But most people do not **appreciate** this fact.

After sleeping all night, your body needs energy.
5 Breakfast gets you ready for your day. Students need breakfast to focus on their **lectures**. And **adults** who eat breakfast aren't hungry at work. Consequently, they won't be tempted[1] to eat unhealthy snacks later in the day.

For a good breakfast, eat lots of fruits and vegetables. They are full of
10 vitamins, which help your body fight diseases. Fruit is delicious and refreshing in the morning, too. Include whole grains[2] in your breakfast. Whole grains give you energy until lunch. That's because your body digests[3] them slowly. As a result, you feel full longer. Here are some **intelligent** breakfast choices:

- low-fat yogurt with lots of fresh fruit

15 • whole-grain oatmeal with apples, pears, or raisins

- a vegetable omelet

- whole-grain muffins filled with nuts or fruits

---

[1] *tempted:* to want to do something that is not good for you
[2] *whole grains:* foods such as rice, oats, or wheat with no part of the food removed
[3] *digest:* to change food in your stomach so your body can use the nutrients

And **remove** sweet cereals and fatty donuts from your house. Make healthy foods **available** instead.

THE BAD AND THE BETTER ABOUT FAT

20 Everyone needs healthy fats. That's right, fat can be good for you!

You probably know all about the bad fats, or trans fats. You find them in meat and in dairy products such as cheese and butter. Trans fats are used to
25 deep-fry French fries and other junk food such as donuts. Trans fats are unhealthy because they increase your cholesterol level. High cholesterol levels can cause heart disease.

But did you know about the good fats? Fats that are found in olive oil, fish,
30 and nuts? These fats can actually lower your cholesterol level. They also boost[4] your immune system,[5] which keeps you healthy. You even need fat to benefit from vitamins. Because some important vitamins stay in your fat, they are always **available** for your body.

So replace a bad fat like butter with a better fat like olive oil, and keep healthy.

SAY NO TO SUGAR

35 "Mom, can I have a cookie?!"

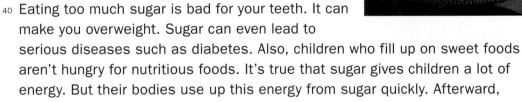

Every **adult** has heard this before. The sound of a child who wants a sugary snack. You might think giving a child a cookie is a **minor** thing. But many parents don't **appreciate** all the dangers of sugar.

40 Eating too much sugar is bad for your teeth. It can make you overweight. Sugar can even lead to serious diseases such as diabetes. Also, children who fill up on sweet foods aren't hungry for nutritious foods. It's true that sugar gives children a lot of energy. But their bodies use up this energy from sugar quickly. Afterward,
45 children feel more tired than before.

So keep your children from eating too much sugar. It may not make them happy. But it will make them healthy.

For a **chart** that lists the sugar content of common snacks, visit the National Health Institute website and use the keyword *sugar*—that's *S-U-G-A-R*.

---

[4] *boost:* to increase or make stronger
[5] *immune system:* the system in your body that protects you from sickness and disease

WRITING SKILL — Cause and Effect

LEARN

PSA script writers try to persuade people to make good decisions. PSAs often name the positive and negative effects of an action. When you write about causes and effects, connect your ideas with words and phrases such as *because, so, as a result, consequently,* and *which can cause.*

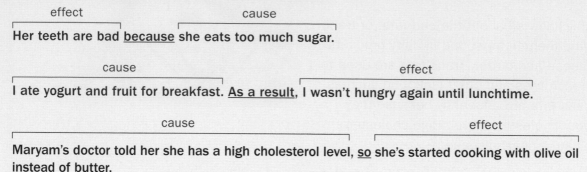

effect   cause

Her teeth are bad <u>because</u> she eats too much sugar.

cause   effect

I ate yogurt and fruit for breakfast. <u>As a result</u>, I wasn't hungry again until lunchtime.

cause   effect

Maryam's doctor told her she has a high cholesterol level, <u>so</u> she's started cooking with olive oil instead of butter.

Include these elements in a persuasive PSA using examples of cause and effect:

1. Describe to the audience what you want them to do.

2. Tell why or what will happen if they follow your advice.

3. Explain what will happen if the audience does not follow your advice.

4. Summarize these causes and effects at the end of your script.

APPLY

A. Read *Say No to Sugar* on page 101 again. With a partner, complete the summary below with the words and phrases in the box.

as a result	because	cause	so

Sugar makes children feel full. (1) _____, they don't want nutritious

foods. Eating sugar often can even (2) _____ diseases such as

diabetes. Foods with a lot of sugar give children energy. But later they feel

weaker (3) _____ energy from sugar lasts for only a short time.

Parents should be sure children eat healthy food (4) _____ that

they will have energy all day.

B. Read *The Bad and the Better about Fat* on page 101 again. Complete the chart below with causes and effects. Compare your answers with a partner.

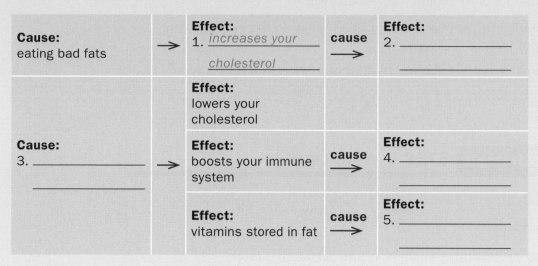

Cause: eating bad fats	→	Effect: 1. *increases your* *cholesterol*	cause →	Effect: 2. _____ _____
		Effect: lowers your cholesterol		
Cause: 3. _____ _____	→	Effect: boosts your immune system	cause →	Effect: 4. _____ _____
		Effect: vitamins stored in fat	cause →	Effect: 5. _____ _____

Analyze

A. Read the PSAs on pages 100–101 again. Check (✓) the information in the chart below that is included in each PSA. With a partner, underline examples of this information in the PSA.

Type of information	Breakfast: Not a Minor Meal	The Bad and the Better about Fat	Say No to Sugar
1. Clear advice for the audience	✓	✓	✓
2. Positive effects of following the advice			
3. Negative effects of not following the advice			
4. Specific suggestions of foods that are good for you			
5. Places to get more information			

B. PSAs usually have a concluding statement with a memorable final idea. Underline the conclusion of each PSA on pages 100–101. With a partner, circle the method below that it uses. One PSA uses both methods.

1. *Breakfast: Not a Minor Meal*

   summarizes the advice   gives additional advice

2. *The Bad and the Better about Fat*

   summarizes the advice   gives additional advice

3. *Say No to Sugar*

   summarizes the advice   gives additional advice

C. Discuss these questions in a small group.

1. Why do writers use PSAs to explain important issues?

2. What is the main idea or purpose of each PSA? What do the writers want the audience to do?

3. PSAs are very short. What are the advantages of a short announcement?

4. How would information in the PSAs be presented differently in a longer article or essay?

Vocabulary Activities | STEP I: Word Level

Available means "ready to use, have, or see."

> *Fresh fruit will be **available** in the summer.*

Follow *available* with prepositions such as *to* and *for* to give more information.

The phrase *available to* tells who can use something.

> *The study room is **available** to all students at the university.*

The phrase *available for* tells the purpose of something.

> *Discounted hotel rooms are **available** for people attending the conference.*

A. Complete the sentences below with *available*, *available to*, or *available for*.

1. A new brand of organic meals will be _____*available*_____ next week.

2. These meals will be _____ families with children ages one to 17.

3. The company wants these meals to be _____ all over the country.

4. If we make healthy food _____ everyone, more people will eat healthily.

5. Also, a book is _____ educating people about eating well.

The adjective *intelligent* describes "being able to think, learn, and understand well." The adverb form is *intelligently*, and the noun form is *intelligence*.

> *The students are very **intelligent**. They always get high scores on their tests.*

> *Joanna works **intelligently**. She finishes easy tasks first, so she can focus on harder ones.*

> *You need **intelligence** to solve the puzzles in the newspaper.*

B. Complete the sentences below with the correct form of the word *intelligent*.
Work with a partner.

1. It is very difficult to make a test that shows how _____*intelligent*_____ people are.

2. Intellect or _____ is an idea that is very hard to define.

3. I admire how she solves problems _____ and quickly.

4. Some people say experience is more important than _____.

5. In any case, we all agree that acting _____ is better than acting carelessly.

C. Work with a partner to complete the paragraph with the words in the box.
Change the form of the words if necessary.

adults	chart	lecture	minor

I just heard a (1) _____ that said coffee can be good for you. It may

help prevent serious illnesses. Coffee can also prevent (2) _____

problems that are not serious. And it tastes good! However, it may only be

healthy for (3) _____, not children. In my opinion, coffee shops

should create a (4) _____ showing how much coffee is safe for

people of different ages to drink.

Vocabulary Activities STEP II: Sentence Level

D. Complete the sentences with advice for parents who want to feed their children
healthy food. Use the words in parentheses.

1. Be sure that fruit _____*is available for children to eat*_____. (available)

2. You need to teach children to _____ the importance of
_____. (appreciate)

3. To avoid eating sugar, _____. (remove)

4. You can find nutritional information _____. (chart)

To appreciate something means "to enjoy it because you understand its good qualities."

> We **appreciate** the restaurant's fresh and delicious food.

To appreciate can also mean "to be thankful for something."

> I really **appreciated** your help when I moved to my new home.

To appreciate has a third meaning. It can mean "to understand that something is true."

> I **appreciate** that it was difficult for you to find time to meet with me.

E. Rewrite the sentences below using the word *appreciate*. Work with a partner.

1. Many people don't know that cooking healthy food is easy.

   Many people don't appreciate that cooking healthy food is easy.

2. We are thankful for how hard you worked to make this delicious dinner.

   _____

3. My friend grew up on a farm, so he really enjoys the taste of a fresh apple.

   _____

4. A small gift is a good way to show you are thankful for your friends.

   _____

5. I understand that unhealthy food may still taste delicious.

   _____

Minor means "not important, not serious, or not dangerous."

> Bob played a **minor** role in the project. He did not do most of the work.

> I got a **minor** cut on my finger.

The opposite of *minor* is *major*.

F. Write sentences giving minor and major examples of each word or phrase.

1. edits to an essay

   Correcting the spelling is a minor edit.

   Revising the introduction and conclusion is a major edit.

2. journey

   _____

   _____

3. surgery

   _____

   _____

4. change in eating habits

   _____

   _____

   _____

Grammar *This* and *That*

The words *this*, *that*, *these*, and *those* are pronouns. They refer to people or things.

Use *this* to refer to a person or thing near you. The plural form is *these*.

<u>This</u> is a warm hat that I'm wearing.   <u>These</u> books that I'm carrying are new.

Use *that* to point out a person or thing that is far away. The plural form is *those*.

<u>That</u> is the school over there.   <u>Those</u> trees up on the hill are apple trees.

That and *those* can also refer to people and things from the past.

<u>That</u> was a very funny movie.   <u>Those</u> people we met were nice.

A. Fill in the blanks below with *this, that, these,* or *those*. Check your answers with a partner.

1. _____*This*_____ is a nice painting that I am looking at.

2. _____ were colorful flowers that we saw yesterday.

3. _____ is the man I met this morning. He's standing over there.

4. _____ are my friends, Jordan and Edward.

5. _____ are beautiful plants and flowers over there.

B. Work with a partner. Write four sentences describing things that are near you right now. Then write four sentences describing things in the classroom that are far away from you. Use *this*, *that*, *these*, and *those* as needed.

This is my favorite pen because it writes very well.

Those books on the shelf are very big.

This, These

1. _____

2. _____

3. _____

4. _____

That, Those

5. _____

6. _____

7. _____

8. _____

C. Some of the sentences below have errors with *this*, *that*, *these*, or *those*. Find the errors and write the correct word. The first sentence has been corrected for you.

This

1. ~~These~~ new restaurant is great. I'm glad we came here.

2. That are beautiful tomatoes you are growing here.

3. That look like interesting cookbooks on the shelf over there.

4. These cookbooks are about Indian food. This over there are about Mexican food.

5. Where did you put this apples?

6. This meal last night was delicious.

7. Is this your car down the street?

8. That is a lovely park. Should we stop and have our picnic right here?

WRITING SKILL   Hooks

LEARN

A hook is a way to get your readers' attention. PSAs are very short. You only have a short amount of time to make your audience interested in your advice. Write a hook in the first sentence of the PSA, using one of these strategies.

- Humor, such as a joke or a funny comment:

  If you eat too many oranges, you can turn orange! But one orange a day won't do that.

- An interesting question:

  Why do people eat foods that aren't good for them?

- A surprising fact or opinion about the topic:

  Eating a little chocolate can be healthy.

APPLY

A. Read the model PSAs on pages 100–101 again. Underline the hooks. With a partner, match each PSA with the strategy it uses to get readers' attention.

___ *Breakfast: Not a Minor Meal*	a. humor
___ *The Bad and the Better about Fats*	b. interesting question
___ *Say No to Sugar*	c. surprising fact

B. Work in a small group. Read the advice below and choose two pieces of advice that you believe are important. For each one, think of a hook for an imaginary PSA promoting that advice.

be on time to class	obey traffic laws
exercise regularly	volunteer your time to a good cause

Advice: *be on time to class*

Hook: *Is your name "Late?" Then why does the teacher always say "Late" when you come to class?*

Advice: _____

Hook: _____

Advice: _____

Hook: _____

Collaborative Writing

A. Look at the information in the chart below about the health benefits of apples. Underline the target words.

Facts about apples	Benefits
Apples have pectin.	Pectin lowers the cholesterol that can cause heart disease.
Apples have vitamin C.	Vitamin C helps your immune system. That keeps you from getting sick.
Applies have antioxidants.	Antioxidants can improve your memory and intelligence.
Apples are firm.	The texture can remove some minor stains from your teeth.

B. Imagine you are going to write a PSA about the benefits of eating apples. With a partner, write a hook you believe will get people's attention.

_____ .

C. With your partner, write sentences for a PSA about apples. Connect each fact about apples with a benefit. Use the words or phrases in the box to make the cause-and-effect relationships clear.

as a result	because	consequently	so	which can cause

1. _Apples have pectin. As a result, apples lower cholesterol._ _____

2. _____

3. _____

4. _____

D. Combine your hook and sentences. Share your short PSA with the class. Discuss these questions as a class.

1. What strategy did you use for your hook?

2. Did the hook catch your listeners' attention?

3. Are the cause-and-effect relationships clear?

4. Did the PSA change your opinion of apples?

Independent Writing

A. You will write a script for a PSA that gives advice about nutrition. Think of a way people can eat more healthily.

B. Brainstorm the positive effects of following your advice. Complete the cause-effect graphic organizer below.

Advice		Effect
	→	
	→	
	→	

C. Complete the sentences to help describe what will happen if people don't follow your advice.

Eating too few _____

can _____. That's bad

for your _____.

D. Look at the adjectives below. They refer to foods that are good or bad for you. Find the words in the writing models and write down what foods or kind of food they describe.

Good	Foods	Bad	Foods
healthy	*fats in olive oil*	unhealthy	*fats in cheese*
nutritious		junk	
delicious		deep-fried	
whole-grain		sugary	

E. Read the adjectives for good and bad foods in activity D again. Circle the ones you can use in your PSA.

F. Write your PSA. Start with a hook. Use your cause-and-effect outline from activity B and your sentences from activity C. Include adjectives that describe foods and the target vocabulary from page 99.

REVISE AND EDIT

A. Read your PSA. Answer the questions below, and make revisions to your PSA as needed.

1. Check (✓) the information you included in your PSA.

   ☐ hook   ☐ useful information

   ☐ effects of following advice   ☐ concluding statement

   ☐ effects of not following advice ☐ where to get more information

2. Look at the information you did not include. Would adding that information make your PSA better?

Grammar for Editing | Punctuation

Using punctuation correctly is important to make your meaning clear. Statements in English must end with a period (.), not a comma (,).

> **I am from Vietnam. Vietnamese food is often full of vegetables, so it is very healthy.**

Questions end with a question mark (?).

> **When do you usually eat breakfast?**

Use a question mark only at the end of questions, not statements.

> **I want to know where you learned to cook so well.**

> **Where did you learn to cook so well?**

Quotation marks (" ") show exactly what someone said. Use a comma to introduce the words someone said. The punctuation at the end of the sentence goes inside the quotation marks.

> **The professor said, "Study your notes to prepare for the test."**

B. Check the language in your PSA. Revise and edit as needed.

Language Checklist
☐ I used target words in my PSA.
☐ I used adjectives to describe food.
☐ I used *this/that/these/those* correctly.
☐ I used punctuation correctly.

C. Check your PSA again. Repeat activities A and B.

Self-Assessment Review: Go back to page 99 and reassess your knowledge of the target vocabulary. How has your understanding of the words changed? What words do you feel most comfortable using now?

UNIT 9

Painting a Story

In this unit, you will

> analyze reviews and learn how they are used to describe artwork.

> use descriptive writing.

> increase your understanding of the target academic words for this unit.

WRITING SKILLS

> Descriptive Language

> Expressing an Opinion

> **GRAMMAR** Combining Sentences with *Because*

Self-Assessment

Think about how well you know each target word, and check (✓) the appropriate column. I have…

TARGET WORDS	never seen the word before.	heard or seen the word but am not sure what it means.	heard or seen the word and understand what it means.	used the word confidently in *either* speaking or writing.
AWL				
🔑 author				
🔑 chapter				
🔑 culture				
🔑 display				
🔑 grade				
🔑 media				
🔑 status				
🔑 tradition				

🔑 Oxford 3000™ keywords

Building Knowledge

Read these questions. Discuss your answers in a small group.

1. What types of art do you enjoy most?

2. What kinds of public art, such as paintings or sculptures, have you seen?

3. How do you think art affects a space? Think of a place you know that has art. Would that place seem different to you without the art?

Writing Model

An art review informs readers about important or popular works of art. Read about a mural, or wall painting, in a school in California, U.S.A.

Beautiful Mural Gets Students Reading

"Reading takes you to the stars." That's the message of a bright new mural on **display** at Longfellow High School. The mural illustrates an essay
5 about reading. The essay, **authored by** seventh-**grade** student Hiro Tanaka, won the school essay contest last year. Our school supports local artists and **authors**. Because of this **tradition**, the principal hired painter James
10 Rivera to paint the mural. Rivera's **status** as a creative and skilled painter is well-known. This mural has been getting a lot of **media** attention. And it should.

Rivera knows how to compose a mural. He
15 laid out the different parts of it so that the message is clear. The scene of the mural is very dynamic,[1] very exciting. Five children are standing on top of books in a dark blue sky. The enormous books catch your attention in
20 the front of the scene. Their important **status** is unmistakable.[2] The five children are from different **cultures**. These children represent the many different **cultures** in our city and schools. The children hold hands as they stand in a

The mural "Reading Takes You to the Stars."
Medium: acrylic paints

25 circle. The large Earth floats beneath the children as they fly in the night sky. The sky **displays** bright white stars behind the children. A large orange sun is on the left side. A cheerful white moon is on the right.
30 I really like how colorful the mural is. And how dynamic it is, too. It's like the children are

---

[1] *dynamic:* full of energy and ideas
[2] *unmistakable:* clear, obvious, or easy to understand

actually moving. Personally, I think that the bright colors highlight a positive message: Reading is the best way to open your mind.

35 "The mural has lots of stars because stars represent goals," said Rivera. "And in my **culture**, the sun means hope. The moon means dreams." Indeed, books can help you achieve your goals. Reading gives you hope. And reading

40 teaches you to dream.

I believe that this message applies[3] to students of all backgrounds[4] in all **grades**. I particularly like the way the children fly above the world. To me, this means that reading takes

45 you outside of your world. You can read about other people, other places, other **traditions**.

Rivera also notes, "Usually books have a title and **author** on the cover. As any book can improve your mind, I painted blank books."

50 That is an important lesson.

I feel one thing is missing, though. Because of the school setting, I was surprised the mural does not also include teachers. Teachers also give students hopes and dreams,

55 after all. But perhaps in the end, reading is more important since school is only one **chapter** in life. Reading lasts forever.

[3] *apply (to):* to be about someone or something, or important to someone or something
[4] *background:* the culture of your family, or where you come from

Descriptive Language

LEARN

Art reviews have descriptive language to help the reader picture, or imagine, what the artwork looks like. Descriptive language gives details.

Use these strategies to write with descriptive language:

- Do not use general adjectives such as *good* or *bad* or *beautiful*. Be specific about what you like or don't like: *colorful, bright, cheerful, interesting, dull, dark, sad,* or *boring*.

- Use adjectives to describe everything about the art. Describe the size, shape, and color of different parts of the art. Tell what is interesting or different about this artwork.

  *The painting shows **large, bright yellow sunflowers in sunlight**.*

- Use specific nouns. It is better to say *tiger* rather than *animal*, or *child* rather than *person*.

- Explain the relationship between things. Tell where things are.

  *The small white mouse **is running away** from the large, dark brown cat. The cat **is behind** the mouse and **on top of** the green wooden table.*

APPLY

A. Read the second paragraph of the art review on page 114 again. Look for descriptive language while you read. Work with a partner to complete the following activities.

1. Circle all the adjectives.

2. Underline the noun that each adjective describes.

3. Discuss the meaning of each adjective, or what it tells the reader about the noun.

B. Read the third paragraph of the art review on pages 114–115 again. Find adjectives in that paragraph to complete the paragraph below that describes the mural.

The mural has many beautiful colors. It is very (1) _____. The

children look like they are actually moving. The scene is very

(2) _____. The colors are very (3) _____ against the

dark night sky. The mural has a (4) _____ message.

Analyze

A. Read the art review on pages 114–115 again. Work with a partner. Answer the questions below. To the left of each question, write the number of the paragraph where you found your answer.

__2__ 1. Who is in the mural? _The mural shows five children standing on books._

____ 2. Does the writer like the mural's colors? _____

____ 3. What does the writer dislike about the mural? _____

____ 4. Who painted the mural and why? _____

____ 5. What is the message in the mural? _____

B. Read the second and third paragraphs of the review on pages 114–115 again. Match the parts of the mural with their meaning. There is one extra meaning. With a partner, discuss what language helped you answer the questions.

__a__ 1. the books   a. the importance of reading

____ 2. standing children   b. hope

____ 3. sun   c. dreams

____ 4. moon   d. the different cultures of children in the school

____ 5. stars   e. goals

      f. teachers in the school

C. Summarize the message of the whole mural in your own words below. Compare your summary with a partner.

_____

_____

_____

D. Discuss these questions in a small group.

1. Which sentence is the hook? What method does the hook use to get the reader's attention?

2. Introductions give important background information. What information about the mural does the author include in the first paragraph?

3. Reviewers sometimes include their opinion in the introduction. Which sentences tell you the reviewer likes this mural?

4. Is there any other information you would like to know about the mural that the writer does not include?

A. Complete the chart below with the correct forms of the target words in the box. Use a dictionary to check your answers.

| author | chapter | display | grade | status |

Word Form Chart			
Noun	**Verb**	**Adjective**	**Adverb**
author		_____	_____
	_____	_____	_____
display		displayed	_____
			_____
	_____	_____	_____

B. Fill in the missing words in the paragraph with the correct form of the words from activity A.

Don't miss the (1) _____*display*_____ of books at the library this month! It

focuses on books by famous British (2) _____. Some of the writers

include Charles Dickens, Jane Austen, and Charlotte Brontë. The exhibit

(3) _____ the original parts of books that are handwritten. There

is even a whole (4) _____ of the book *Oliver Twist*. It was also

interesting to hear about the fame and (5) _____ of authors 100

years ago. It's different from how they are seen today.

C. Complete the sentences below with the words in parentheses. Compare your answers with a partner.

1. Sarah goes to _____*school*_____. She is in the fourth _____*grade*_____.
   (grade/school)

2. The _____ gave _____ to all the students' essays.
   (teacher/grades)

3. At home, teachers _____ for their classes and _____
   student work. (grade/prepare)

4. The teacher handed back all of the _____ _____.
   (essays/graded)

Status means "the condition of a thing or person at a particular time."

What is the **status** of your essay? Have you finished it yet?

Status can also refer to "the social or professional position of a person or group."

Doctors usually have high **status** because they have a lot of education and do important work.

Status can also refer to "the official or legal position of a person or group."

In many countries, people who are 18 years old have the legal **status** of adults.

CORPUS

D. Rewrite the sentences below using the word *status*. Check your answers with a partner.

1. My boss wants to know the condition of the project.

   My boss wants to know the status of the project.
   _____

2. In many countries, famous people have a high social position.

   _____

3. They gave him the position of team captain.

   _____

4. After he got his master's degree, his position at work increased.

   _____

5. The doctor told the patient's family how he was doing. She said he was doing much better.

   _____

A *medium* can refer to "the materials that a piece of art is made out of." In this meaning, the plural is either *mediums* or *media*.

*The **media** of the sculpture are clay and metal.*

The noun *medium* can also refer to "a form of communication such as television, radio, the Internet, and newspapers." In this meaning, the plural is *media*. This type of *media* is sometimes used with a singular verb.

*I get news from different **media** sources.*

*The **media** usually covers the president's speeches.*

E. Use the different media types in the box to write sentences that answer the questions. Use *media* in your answers. Then compare your answers in a small group.

the Internet	magazine	movies	newspaper	radio	television

1. Which media do you use to get news?

   My favorite news media are television and the Internet.

2. What are the best media sources for sports?

   _____

3. Which media do you pay attention to most?

   _____

4. Which media do you use least?

   _____

Culture means "the customs, art, ideas, and way of life of a group of people." The adjective form is *cultural*.

*When I travel to a different country, I always want to learn about the **culture** there.*

Tradition means "a belief or habit that a group of people have had for a long time." The adjective form is *traditional*.

*This is a **traditional** dress that was worn in my country many years ago.*

F. Describe two holidays in your country or in another country you know about. Which culture celebrates the holiday? Then write a traditional thing people do on that holiday, and the cultural meaning of that tradition. Work with a partner.

Holiday: *Chuseok is a holiday celebrated in the Korean culture in the fall.*

Tradition: *It is a tradition for families to eat a big meal on Chuseok.*

Cultural meaning: *Eating together shows the cultural importance of families in Korea.*

1. Holiday: _____

Tradition: _____

Cultural meaning: _____

2. Holiday: _____

Tradition: _____

Cultural meaning: _____

Grammar Combining Sentences with *Because*

Use *because* to combine two sentences. The conjunction *because* introduces the reason why a situation happens.

Place a comma after the reason when *because* begins the sentence.

reason   situation

<u>Because</u> Tim lives outside the city, he takes the train into the city.

Do not use a comma when *because* introduces the reason in the middle of the sentence.

reason   situation

Margarita was late to work <u>because</u> there was a lot of traffic.

Use a subject pronoun in the second part of the sentence when the reason and the situation have the same noun.

Because Miguel is a pilot, <u>he</u> flies to many countries.

A. Complete the sentences below with your own details. Compare your answers with a partner.

1. Because I want to learn English, *I read a book every week in English* .

2. Because it rained yesterday, _____ .

3. _____ because I will be on vacation next week.

4. I run in the park every day because _____

B. Combine the two sentences into one sentence using *because*. Keep the order of the situation and reason the same. Add commas and use subject pronouns where necessary.

1. The sculpture was large (reason)
   It took ten men to lift it. (situation)

   Because the sculpture was large, it took ten men to lift it.

2. We went to the museum. (situation)
   There was a new show there. (reason)

   _____

3. Abbas is an art reviewer. (reason)
   Abbas goes to a lot of art shows. (situation)

   _____

4. The museum is displaying that artist's paintings. (situation)
   This artist was born in our city. (reason)

   _____

5. The mayor wants to make the square more beautiful. (reason)
   The mayor will hire an artist to paint a mural in the square. (situation)

   _____

C. Work with a partner. Read the paragraph below. Correct the errors. You may add *because* at the beginning or middle of a sentence. You may add or cross out a comma. You may also change a capital letter to a lowercase letter.

Because art

Personally, I enjoy looking at new art, but some people do not. ~~Art~~

can have many meanings, it can be difficult to understand. Some people

think that art is boring the message is often hard to see. In fact, the fun

of looking at art is making up your own mind. People are becoming less

interested in art they visit art museums less and less. But everyone should

go to see more art it can make you think and feel new things.

WRITING SKILL | Expressing an Opinion

LEARN

When you review a piece of art, you give your opinion about it. This includes discussing what you like about the piece as well as what you don't like. A description tells about aspects of the piece that everyone will see the same way. An opinion tells your personal feelings about the piece.

Use a variety of phrases to give your opinion.

> **In my opinion,** *movies based on true stories are the best.*
>
> **I believe that** *this author writes amazing stories.*
>
> **To me,** *Shakespeare's best play is* Hamlet.
>
> **Personally,** *I think that the new mural is dull.*

APPLY

A. Read the sentences below. Write *D* if the statement is a description and *O* if the statement is an opinion.

_D_ 1. The green light shines throughout the piece.

____ 2. It's a glamorous dress.

____ 3. The child's face is as bright as the flower.

____ 4. The colors are plain and boring.

____ 5. The artist painted the lines on the man's tired face with great skill.

B. Rewrite the opinion statements in activity A using a phrase from the Learn section.

_____

_____

_____

_____

C. Read the review on pages 114–115 again. Follow these steps with a partner.

1. Underline the opinion statements in the art review.

2. Tell your partner in your own words what the author's opinion is.

3. Discuss the reasons the author gives for his or her opinion.

Collaborative Writing

A. Look at the painting *Starry Night* by Vincent Van Gogh. Work with a partner. Agree on three things you like and three things you don't like about it. You may talk about the colors, the items in the painting, the style, or its meaning.

Like	Dislike
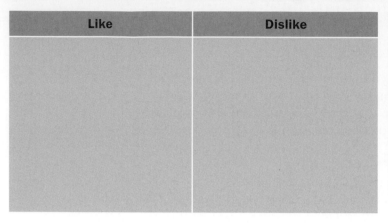	

Starry Night by Vincent Van Gogh

B. Choose the three opinions from activity A that you and your partner feel most strongly about. They can be positive or negative.

1. Write three sentences using different opinion phrases.

   a. _____

   b. _____

   c. _____

2. For each opinion, give a reason.

   a. _____

   b. _____

   c. _____

3. Write one or more concluding sentences that give your and your partner's overall opinion of the painting. Do you like it or dislike it?

C. Share your sentences with the class. Discuss these questions.

1. What about the painting does the class like?

2. What about the painting does the class dislike?

Independent Writing

A. You are going to write an art review. Think of a piece of art that you know well. It could be a mural or sculpture in your town, or a famous piece of art. It could be a painting, a piece of pottery, or a drawing that you are familiar with.

Piece of art: _____

B. Write an outline of your review. Answer the questions in the chart as a guide.

First paragraph	1. What type of artwork is it? 2. Who made it and why?
Second paragraph	3. What people or things does the artwork show? 4. What words describe its shape, size, and colors?
Third paragraph	5. Does the artwork have a message? 6. Why is this artwork interesting or important?

C. Circle the adjectives of color below that describe the artwork you are reviewing.

blue	cool	dull	light	purple	warm
bright	dark	green	orange	red	yellow

VOCABULARY TIP

Adjectives that describe colors and sizes make descriptions of art more vivid.

D. Include your opinion in your review. Complete the sentences as a guide.

1. I like this piece of art because _____.

2. I believe that the most interesting part is _____.

   I think this because _____.

3. In my opinion, the message of this art is _____.

4. Personally, I think that _____

   could be better. I believe this since _____.

5. To me, this artwork is important because _____.

E. Write your review. Use your answers from activity B to organize your ideas. Use sentences that you like from activity D. As you write, include adjectives of color and size as well as the target vocabulary on page 113.

REVISE AND EDIT

A. Read your art review. Answer the questions below, and make revisions to your review as needed.

1. Check (✓) the information you included in your review.

   ☐ description of the artwork   ☐ background information

   ☐ what you like   ☐ message of the artwork

   ☐ reasons for your opinions   ☐ what you don't like

2. Look at the information you did not include. Would adding that information make your review more informative?

Grammar for Editing   Avoiding Fragments

A sentence without a subject or verb is called a *fragment*. Fragments are not complete sentences. Use complete sentences in formal writing.

Some fragments are missing the verb.

>   is
> It ^ great to be at the beach today.

Some fragments have a dependent clause without an independent clause. Fix this type of fragment by using a comma instead of a period.

>   , such
> My brother likes a lot of sports. ~~Such~~ as soccer, hockey, and handball.

B. Check the language in your review. Revise and edit as needed.

Language Checklist
☐ I used target words in my review.
☐ I used adjectives that describe colors.
☐ I used *because* correctly in sentences.
☐ I used only complete sentences, not fragments.

C. Check your review again. Repeat activities A and B.

Self-Assessment Review: Go back to page 113 and reassess your knowledge of the target vocabulary. How has your understanding of the words changed? What words do you feel most comfortable using now?

UNIT
10

Greening Our Cities

In this unit, you will

> analyze a persuasive letter and how it is used in newspapers and media websites.
> use argumentative writing.
> increase your understanding of the target academic words for this unit.

WRITING SKILLS

> Arguing an Opinion
> Parallel Structure
> **GRAMMAR** Negatives

Self-Assessment

Think about how well you know each target word, and check (✓) the appropriate column. I have...

TARGET WORDS	never seen the word before.	heard or seen the word but am not sure what it means.	heard or seen the word and understand what it means.	used the word confidently in *either* speaking or writing.
AWL				
🔑 depress				
🔑 document				
🔑 draft				
🔑 file				
🔑 found				
🔑 publish				
🔑 symbol				
🔑 text				

🔑 Oxford 3000™ keywords

Building Knowledge

Read these questions. Discuss your answers in a small group.

1. Do you like going to parks or places in nature?

2. Do you think it is important for cities to have parks in them or near them?

3. Would you ever write an online letter about a public topic?

Writing Model

Persuasive letters in the media are often called letters to the editor. They make an argument about an issue and encourage readers to do something, or to take an action. Read a persuasive letter about protecting a greenbelt, which is an area of nature that surrounds a city.

Vote No to Development on the Branhaven Greenbelt!

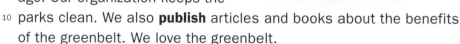

Dear Sir or Madam:

As an ecologist, I chose to live in Branhaven because of the beautiful greenbelt. This series of
5 parks surrounding the town is a good balance to Branhaven's urban areas. I **founded** Friends of the Branhaven Greenbelt two years ago. Our organization keeps the
10 parks clean. We also **publish** articles and books about the benefits of the greenbelt. We love the greenbelt.

So I was **depressed** to read that the town council[1] wants to destroy[2] it. They have **drafted** a law to allow building on the greenbelt. We will not let this law pass.

15 The city planners say this law will benefit the economy of Branhaven. It will mean jobs and new businesses. However, it will

---

[1] *council:* a group of people who are chosen to work together and make rules
[2] *destroy:* to break something so completely that you cannot use it again

also destroy the environment. And the environment is important for wildlife, for Branhaven residents, and for Branhaven businesses.

20 First, the greenbelt does keep the Branhaven economy strong. Tourists hear about the greenbelt and visit it. People in the park buy water, snacks, and maps. There are also restaurants and shops on the streets next to the park. Those local businesses rely on the greenbelt to
25 attract customers.

Second, the greenbelt keeps the air fresh. Trees and plants take in polluting gases and clean the air. A recent study showed there was
30 more air pollution before the greenbelt. The greenbelt also keeps many factories from being built around our town. More factories would mean more
35 air pollution.

Most importantly, the greenbelt makes our town a nice place to live. The greenbelt is a **symbol** of what I love about Branhaven. The last time I went there, I saw beautiful spring flowers coming up, I saw ducks swimming in the lake, and I saw families with
40 children playing. The sounds of city traffic didn't reach us. Without this green resource, the city will be a sadder place.

I ask you to take action. Educate yourself. Read the law the city councilors want to pass. A **draft** of the law was **published** in last week's *Branhaven Times*. And the full **text** of the law can be
45 downloaded as a PDF **file** from the town website. After you read the law, read the **document** *Save the Greenbelt* on our website. It will explain our opinion.

And finally, write the city council to tell them to drop this plan. We have **drafted** sample letters you can use. Just go to our website
50 to find several points to discuss in your letter. Copy and paste any **text** you like.

Remember, the future of our town is in your hands.

Sincerely,

James Wilson

55 **Founder**, Friends of the Branhaven Greenbelt

WRITING SKILL Arguing an Opinion

LEARN

The purpose of a persuasive letter is to convince readers to do something you want them to do. When writing a persuasive letter, support your opinion with reasons. Explain each reason with examples or facts. This will help readers see your point of view.

Before you argue an opinion, follow these steps:

1. Write each reason you have for your opinion.

2. Organize your reasons in order of importance. Explain your least important reason first and your most important reason last. This leaves readers thinking about the strongest argument.

3. Use details, such as facts and examples, to support your reasons.

4. You may include reasons why the opinion that is the opposite of your argument is weak, or not good. This can show why your opinion is better. It can also cause people who disagree with you to change their minds.

APPLY

A. Read the letter to the editor on pages 128–129 again. The writer gives three reasons why the greenbelt should be protected. Complete the sentences below to name each reason.

1. The greenbelt is an important part of the local _____economy_____.

2. The greenbelt cleans the _____.

3. The greenbelt improves the quality of the whole _____.

B. Match the examples or facts below with the reasons from activity A. Write *1*, *2*, or *3* next to each example or fact.

__2__ 1. Air pollution has decreased.

_____ 2. Visitors go to the businesses nearby.

_____ 3. Children play there.

_____ 4. Plants absorb pollution.

_____ 5. Tourists like to visit it.

_____ 6. People sell things near it.

_____ 7. It prevents companies from building factories.

_____ 8. Animals can live there.

C. Read the first three paragraphs of the persuasive letter on page 128 again. Which sentence gives the general opinion that the writer supports? Discuss your answer with a partner.

Analyze

A. Read the third paragraph in the letter on page 128 again. This paragraph gives a reason why the other side of the argument is weak. Write the sentences from the third paragraph below with their purpose.

1. statement of the other side's argument

   _____

2. example supporting the other side's argument

   _____

3. something negative about the other side's argument

   _____

4. reasons why the author's opinion is the correct one

   _____

B. With a partner, discuss why this paragraph makes the letter stronger.

C. Persuasive letters often ask people to do something. The letter then gives people resources to help them do it. Circle the correct answer to each question below.

1. Why does the author mention that you can download a copy of the law?

   a. so people can read it

   b. so people can vote on it

   c. so people can edit it

2. Why does the author want people to read *Save the Greenbelt*?

   a. to get it on a best-seller list

   b. to learn more about his opinion

   c. to help elect a candidate

3. Who does the author want the reader to write to?

   a. the Friends of the Branhaven Greenbelt

   b. the city council

   c. the Branhaven greenbelt Business Association

4. What help can you find on the Friends of the Branhaven Greenbelt website?

   a. a map of the greenbelt

   b. a list of addresses

   c. useful phrases to put into a letter

D. Persuasive letters are usually written to a particular group of people who can take action on an issue. Check (✓) the people who might be a part of the writer's intended audience. Discuss your choices with a partner.

___ 1. a teenager who runs in the greenbelt

___ 2. a family that wants to build a house on the greenbelt

___ 3. a town resident who believes in protecting the environment

___ 4. a visitor from another city

___ 5. a member of the city council

Vocabulary Activities STEP I: Word Level

A. Complete the chart below with the correct forms of the target words in the box. Use a dictionary to check your answers.

document	draft	publish	text

Word Form Chart			
Noun	**Verb**	**Adjective**	**Adverb**
document documentation	*document*		_____
			_____
publisher			_____
	_____	textual	_____

B. Complete the paragraph below with the correct forms of the words from activity A. Compare your answers with a partner.

It is easy to write and print your own advertising. Computers have programs

that help you make professional-looking (1) ___documents___ such as

brochures and posters. You can add beautiful illustrations. But the most

important part is the words, or (2) _____. Make sure to write a

first (3) _____ and check it carefully. Then you are ready to

(4) _____ your ad.

The verb *depress* means "to make someone feel unhappy for a long period of time."

*Movies that have sad endings **depress** me and make me cry.*

Depress has two adjective forms. *Depressed* describes someone who feels unhappy for a long period of time. *Depressing* describes something that causes people to feel sad.

*I'm **depressed** because I can't find a job.*

*Rainy weather is **depressing** because it's dark outside.*

 CORPUS

C. Complete the paragraph below with the correct forms of the word *depress*.

Reading that the greenbelt is in danger (1) _____depresses_____ me. The

idea of Branhaven without that area of nature is (2) _____.

Any time I read about another green part of the world disappearing, I feel

(3) _____. Looking at trees and animals makes me feel happy,

but views of buildings and factories are just (4) _____. If this law

passes, and companies are allowed to build in the greenbelt, I think I will be

(5) _____ for awhile.

Vocabulary Activities   STEP II: Sentence Level

D. Work with a partner. For each kind of file, circle two things you might find in it. Then take turns making sentences.

1. a word processing file   a painting / a video game / (an essay) / (a letter)
   A word processing file can contain an essay or a letter.

2. a spreadsheet file   a résumé / a budget / a book / a database
   _____

3. an image file   a website / a recipe / a photograph / a map
   _____

4. a video file   a TV show / a map / a shopping list / a movie
   _____

5. a music file   a test / a song / a magazine article / a lecture
   _____

E. Write sentences to answer the questions below. Use the word *file* as a verb in your answers. Share your answers with a partner.

1. How is your music collection organized?

   I file all of my songs based on the type of music they are.

2. How do store your important identification papers?

   _____

3. How are your school writing assignments arranged in your computer?

   _____

4. Do you have a special way of organizing the photographs on your phone?

   _____

A *founder* is "someone who starts a company or an organization."

   The **founder** of Apple was Steve Jobs.

The verb form is *found*. The past tense is *founded*.

   He **founded** an environmental organization to protect wolves.

C CORPUS

F. Rewrite the sentences below with the form of *found* in parentheses.

1. John started a new company last year. (founded)

   John founded a new company last year.

2. The person who began the Animals Club quit last year. (founder)

   _____

3. In the future, I would like to start my own company. (found)

   _____

4. Some businesspeople create several companies in their lives. (found)

   _____

A *symbol* is "an object, sign, or picture that has a special meaning." When a shape or image means something else, it is a *symbol for* that other thing.

   In a traffic signal, a red light is usually a **symbol** for "stop."

When a *symbol* is associated with an idea or emotion, it is a *symbol of* it. The verb form is *symbolize*.

   The lion is a **symbol** of bravery and strength.

C CORPUS

G. Work with a partner. Match each symbol on the left with its meaning. Then take turns making sentences. Use *symbol* or *symbolize* in each sentence.

_a_ 1. the sun   a. hope

___ 2. a sign with an airplane on it   b. happiness

___ 3. a dove   c. not allowed

___ 4. three arrows forming a triangle   d. an airport

___ 5. a circle with a diagonal line through it   e. recycling

1. _The sun can symbolize hope._ _____

2. _____

3. _____

4. _____

5. _____

Grammar | Negatives

Sentences with different types of verbs become negative in different ways. When a sentence has a simple present verb, add the words *do not* or *does not* before the verb.

> We <u>*do not*</u> support building houses on the green.

> He <u>*does not*</u> like running inside a gym.

When a sentence has a verb in the simple future or past, place the word *not* before the main verb. *Not* will be after auxiliary verbs such as *did, will, can, should,* or *may.*

> The sounds of city traffic <u>*did not*</u> reach us.

When a sentence has the verb *be*, place *not* after *be*.

> I am <u>*not*</u> convinced that the town needs more buildings.

A. Correct the five remaining errors in the paragraph below.

Planning cities is important. A city ~~not does~~ *does not* grow without good

planning. For example, if you put factories next to houses, people not will

want to live there. Also, building houses far from parks not a good idea.

Cities need to balance the needs of businesses and people. One be not more

important than the other. In the past, city planning not was important. Now,

town councils not ignore the importance of planning.

B. Rewrite the sentences so that they are negative.

1. I drink tea every morning.

   I do not drink tea every morning.

2. She went to the store last night.

   _____

3. My brothers and sisters visit me often.

   _____

4. I finished my homework before class began.

   _____

5. Your street is very busy.

   _____

C. Answer the questions below in complete sentences.

1. Did you go to a concert today?

   I did not go to a concert today.

2. Are you flying an airplane right now?

   _____

3. Will you go to the moon tonight?

   _____

4. Are you the King of England?

   _____

5. Do you usually eat lunch at 6 a.m.?

   _____

6. Is two plus two five?

   _____

WRITING SKILL — Parallel Structure

LEARN

Use parallel structure to show that different points in your letter are related to each other and have the same level of importance. You can use parallel structure in words, phrases, or clauses.

1. Use gerunds or infinitives in a sentence, but not both.

   ✗ I enjoy _walking_, _hiking_, and _to ride_ my bike in the city park.

   ✓ I enjoy _walking_, _hiking_, and _bike riding_ in the city park.

2. Use the same form of word to begin each point in a list.

   ✗ People in the park buy _water_, _snacks_, and _take_ park maps.

   ✓ People in the park buy _water_, _snacks_, and _park maps_.

3. Use the same clause to begin related points.

   ✗ Tell the city council that _you want to_ save the greenbelt, _you want to_ keep our city beautiful, and _they should_ vote "no" on the new law.

   ✓ Tell the city council that _you want to_ save the greenbelt, _you want to_ keep our city beautiful, and _you want_ them _to_ vote "no" on the new law.

APPLY

Look at the persuasive letter on pages 128–129 again. Follow the steps below with a partner. Discuss your answers with the class.

1. In the sixth paragraph, underline the sentence that uses parallel structure.

2. In that sentence, circle the words that come after the first two words in each point.

3. Which part of speech are the words you circled?

   _____

4. Why did the writer repeat the same words and part of speech? What effect does using parallel structure have on readers?

   _____

   _____

5. Look at the first sentences of paragraphs four, five, and six. Underline the parts of these sentences that are parallel.

6. Why did the author make these sentences parallel? What role do these three sentences play in the letter?

   _____

   _____

Collaborative Writing

A. Imagine that there is a plan to replace a park with a parking lot in a town you know. Do you think that the park is important for your town? Or do you think that having parking for more cars is more important? Circle your opinion.

A park is better for our town.   A parking lot is better for our town.

B. Find a partner who circled the same opinion as you. Together, create three reasons to support your opinion that you think will be persuasive for your audience. Complete the phrases below to write a basic outline of your argument.

We feel that [opinion] _____ because:

Reason 1: _____

Reason 2: _____

Reason 3: _____

C. Read your outline again. Do you use parallel structure? Revise your outline so that each reason begins with the same word form.

D. With your partner, write the first sentence for each paragraph that will support your argument in a persuasive letter. Use parallel structure to connect the reasons. Put the most important reason last.

_____

_____

_____

_____

_____

E. What action do you want your readers to take after they read your letter?

Reader action: _____

F. Use your opinion statement, three support sentences, and action statement to create a full outline of your argument.

G. Share your outline with the class. Discuss these questions as a class.

1. Were the three reasons clearly related to the opinion statement?

2. Could any of the reasons be replaced with a stronger one?

3. What examples of parallel structure are in the outline?

4. If you had a different opinion, did the argument change your mind?

Independent Writing

A. You are going to write a persuasive letter to a newspaper or other form of news media. Think of something you would like to change in your town. This may be building something new such as a bridge or a new building. It may be repairing a building or adding a traffic sign. Write the problem and your opinion.

I think _____.

B. Brainstorm three reasons for your opinion and one example or detail for each reason. Answer the questions below as a guide.

1. What are three strong reasons for my opinion?

   a. _____

   b. _____

   c. _____

2. Which is the strongest reason? Write the letter here: ____

3. What is an example that will help my audience understand each reason?

   a. _____

   b. _____

   c. _____

C. Circle the phrases you want to use in your letter that show you are expressing an opinion.

| I am certain | I am sure | I believe | I feel | I think |

> **VOCABULARY TIP**
>
> Persuasive letters often include phrases that mean "I think" or "I believe." There are many synonyms for these terms.

D. Finish the sentences below to help you write your opinion clearly.

1. In my opinion, _____ is a

   problem because _____.

2. I think that we need to change _____.

3. If we don't do this, _____.

4. Since _____,

   the town needs to _____.

E. Write your persuasive letter. Use your reasons from activity B. Include any sentences you like from activity D. Use the target vocabulary from page 127. Conclude your letter by naming the action you would like your readers to take.

A. Read your persuasive letter. Answer the questions below, and make revisions to your letter as needed.

1. Check (✓) the information you included in your letter.

   ☐ background information

   ☐ opinion

   ☐ details and support for your reasons

   ☐ action you want the reader to take

   ☐ information about yourself

   ☐ reasons for your opinion

2. Look at the information you did not include. Would adding that information make your persuasive letter better?

Grammar for Editing — Punctuating Lists

Use punctuation to separate the items in a list. Place a comma after each item in the list except for the last item.

> A downtown shopping district will need stores, cafés, walkways, and parking spaces.

Use the words *and* or *or* before the last item on the list.

> Every day I walk, jog, *or* ride my bike in the park.

B. Check the language in your letter. Revise and edit as needed.

Language Checklist
☐ I used target words in my persuasive letter.
☐ I used words that express an opinion.
☐ I used negatives correctly.
☐ I used correct punctuation in sentences containing lists.

C. Check your letter again. Repeat activities A and B.

Self-Assessment Review:
Go back to page 127 and reassess your knowledge of the target vocabulary. How has your understanding of the words changed? What words do you feel most comfortable using now?

The Academic Word List

Words targeted in Level Intro are bold.

Word	Sublist	Location
🔑 abandon	8	L2, U6
abstract	6	L3, U1
academy	5	L2, U8
🔑 **access**	**4**	**L0, U6**
accommodate	9	L3, U6
🔑 accompany	8	L4, U6
accumulate	8	L3, U10
🔑 **accurate**	**6**	**L0, U4**
🔑 **achieve**	**2**	**L0, U1**
🔑 **acknowledge**	**6**	**L0, U7**
🔑 acquire	2	L3, U4
🔑 **adapt**	**7**	**L0, U3**
🔑 adequate	4	L3, U3
adjacent	10	L4, U3
🔑 adjust	5	L4, U6
administrate	2	L4, U10
🔑 **adult**	**7**	**L0, U8**
advocate	7	L4, U4
🔑 affect	2	L1, U2
aggregate	6	L4, U5
🔑 aid	7	L3, U4
albeit	10	L4, U9
allocate	6	L3, U1
🔑 alter	5	L2, U6
🔑 alternative	3	L1, U7
ambiguous	8	L4, U7
amend	5	L4, U1
analogy	9	L4, U2
🔑 analyze	1	L1, U9
🔑 annual	4	L1, U6
🔑 anticipate	9	L2, U5
apparent	4	L2, U5
append	8	L4, U9
🔑 **appreciate**	**8**	**L0, U8**
🔑 approach	1	L1, U2
🔑 appropriate	2	L3, U4
🔑 approximate	4	L2, U1
arbitrary	8	L4, U7
🔑 **area**	**1**	**L0, U6**
🔑 aspect	2	L2, U3
assemble	10	L3, U6
assess	1	L2, U4
assign	6	L3, U9
🔑 **assist**	**2**	**L0, U4**
🔑 assume	1	L3, U4
🔑 assure	9	L3, U9
🔑 **attach**	**6**	**L0, U7**

Word	Sublist	Location
attain	9	L3, U5
🔑 attitude	4	L2, U4
attribute	4	L3, U3
🔑 **author**	**6**	**L0, U9**
🔑 authority	1	L2, U9
automate	8	L2, U5
🔑 **available**	**1**	**L0, U8**
🔑 aware	5	L1, U3
🔑 behalf	9	L4, U1
🔑 benefit	1	L2, U4
bias	8	L4, U2
🔑 bond	6	L4, U9
🔑 brief	6	L2, U4
bulk	9	L3, U1
🔑 capable	6	L3, U7
🔑 capacity	5	L4, U2
🔑 category	2	L2, U3
🔑 cease	9	L2, U8
🔑 challenge	5	L1, U2
🔑 channel	7	L4, U3
🔑 **chapter**	**2**	**L0, U9**
🔑 **chart**	**8**	**L0, U8**
🔑 chemical	7	L2, U10
🔑 circumstance	3	L4, U3
cite	6	L4, U7
🔑 civil	4	L3, U10
clarify	8	L3, U8
🔑 classic	7	L3, U9
clause	5	L3, U3
🔑 **code**	**4**	**L0, U7**
coherent	9	L4, U6
coincide	9	L4, U6
🔑 collapse	10	L3, U6
🔑 colleague	10	L3, U1
commence	9	L2, U9
🔑 comment	3	L1, U5
🔑 commission	2	L4, U2
🔑 commit	4	L2, U2
commodity	8	L4, U10
🔑 communicate	4	L1, U3
🔑 community	2	L1, U4
compatible	9	L2, U3
compensate	3	L4, U8
compile	10	L3, U2
complement	8	L4, U9

🔑 Oxford 3000™ words

Word	Sublist	Location
complex	2	L3, U10
component	3	L3, U3
compound	5	L3, U10
comprehensive	7	L3, U3
comprise	7	L3, U1
compute	2	L1, U7
conceive	10	L4, U4
concentrate	4	L1, U2
concept	1	L3, U9
conclude	**2**	**L0, U2**
concurrent	9	L4, U3
conduct	2	L1, U5
confer	4	L4, U9
confine	9	L4, U4
confirm	7	L1, U10
conflict	5	L1, U10
conform	8	L3, U8
consent	3	L3, U7
consequent	2	L4, U7
considerable	3	L3, U9
consist	1	L1, U1
constant	3	L1, U7
constitute	1	L4, U1
constrain	3	L4, U5
construct	2	L2, U1
consult	5	L2, U2
consume	2	L2, U6
contact	5	L1, U3
contemporary	8	L4, U3
context	1	L2, U4
contract	1	L3, U4
contradict	8	L2, U4
contrary	7	L3, U8
contrast	4	L3, U5
contribute	3	L1, U4
controversy	9	L2, U1
convene	3	L4, U8
converse	9	L2, U10
convert	7	L4, U9
convince	10	L1, U9
cooperate	6	L3, U2
coordinate	3	L2, U5
core	3	L4, U1
corporate	3	L1, U7
correspond	3	L3, U2
couple	**7**	**L0, U7**
create	1	L2, U7
credit	2	L2, U9
criteria	3	L3, U3
crucial	8	L4, U4
culture	**2**	**L0, U9**

Word	Sublist	Location
currency	8	L2, U7
cycle	4	L3, U1
data	**1**	**L0, U3**
debate	4	L3, U5
decade	7	L1, U9
decline	5	L1, U6
deduce	3	L3, U3
define	**1**	**L0, U6**
definite	7	L4, U6
demonstrate	3	L1, U5
denote	8	L4, U10
deny	7	L1, U10
depress	**10**	**L0, U10**
derive	1	L4, U2
design	**2**	**L0, U3**
despite	4	L3, U10
detect	8	L2, U1
deviate	8	L4, U7
device	**9**	**L0, U7**
devote	9	L2, U4
differentiate	7	L3, U8
dimension	4	L4, U9
diminish	9	L2, U6
discrete	5	L4, U10
discriminate	6	L4, U1
displace	8	L3, U5
display	**6**	**L0, U9**
dispose	7	L4, U8
distinct	2	L4, U10
distort	9	L4, U7
distribute	1	L1, U6
diverse	6	L4, U3
document	**3**	**L0, U10**
domain	6	L4, U7
domestic	4	L2, U6
dominate	3	L4, U8
draft	**5**	**L0, U10**
drama	8	L2, U7
duration	9	L2, U5
dynamic	7	L3, U1
economy	1	L2, U3
edit	6	L1, U1
element	2	L3, U9
eliminate	7	L1, U7
emerge	4	L4, U10
emphasis	3	L1, U7
empirical	7	L4, U5
enable	5	L2, U7
encounter	10	L1, U5

⚿ Oxford 3000™ words

Word	Sublist	Location
🔑 **energy**	**5**	**L0, U1**
enforce	5	L4, U7
enhance	6	L3, U5
🔑 **enormous**	**10**	**L0, U2**
🔑 ensure	3	L4, U6
entity	5	L4, U9
🔑 environment	1	L1, U6
equate	2	L3, U2
equip	7	L2, U3
🔑 equivalent	5	L1, U10
erode	9	L4, U8
🔑 **error**	**4**	**L0, U4**
🔑 establish	1	L2, U2
🔑 estate	6	L3, U1
🔑 estimate	1	L2, U8
ethic	9	L3, U8
🔑 ethnic	4	L3, U10
evaluate	2	L1, U8
eventual	8	L3, U5
evident	1	L2, U1
evolve	5	L2, U8
exceed	6	L1, U8
🔑 exclude	3	L2, U2
🔑 exhibit	8	L2, U10
🔑 **expand**	**5**	**L0, U2**
🔑 expert	6	L2, U2
explicit	6	L4, U7
exploit	8	L4, U7
🔑 export	1	L3, U9
🔑 expose	5	L4, U8
external	5	L2, U3
extract	7	L3, U5
facilitate	5	L3, U6
🔑 factor	1	L3, U2
🔑 **feature**	**2**	**L0, U5**
🔑 federal	6	L4, U1
🔑 **fee**	**6**	**L0, U5**
🔑 **file**	**7**	**L0, U10**
🔑 **final**	**2**	**L0, U3**
🔑 finance	1	L3, U4
finite	7	L4, U9
flexible	6	L1, U10
fluctuate	8	L4, U6
🔑 **focus**	**2**	**L0, U1**
format	9	L2, U1
🔑 formula	1	L3, U8
forthcoming	10	L4, U9
🔑 **found**	**9**	**L0, U10**
🔑 foundation	7	L1, U9
framework	3	L4, U3

Word	Sublist	Location
🔑 function	1	L3, U3
🔑 fund	3	L2, U9
🔑 fundamental	5	L1, U8
furthermore	6	L3, U1
gender	6	L3, U2
🔑 generate	5	L1, U4
🔑 generation	5	L2, U8
globe	7	L2, U1
🔑 **goal**	**4**	**L0, U1**
🔑 **grade**	**7**	**L0, U9**
🔑 grant	4	L3, U2
🔑 guarantee	7	L1, U4
guideline	8	L1, U8
hence	4	L3, U1
hierarchy	7	L4, U10
🔑 **highlight**	**8**	**L0, U7**
hypothesis	4	L3, U7
identical	7	L3, U7
🔑 identify	1	L1, U5
ideology	7	L4, U3
ignorance	6	L2, U10
🔑 **illustrate**	**3**	**L0, U6**
🔑 image	5	L1, U7
immigrate	3	L4, U8
🔑 impact	2	L2, U6
implement	4	L4, U7
implicate	4	L3, U7
implicit	8	L4, U1
🔑 imply	3	L3, U5
🔑 impose	4	L3, U8
incentive	6	L4, U5
incidence	6	L3, U2
incline	10	L4, U6
🔑 income	1	L3, U2
incorporate	6	L4, U3
🔑 index	6	L4, U8
🔑 indicate	1	L2, U3
🔑 **individual**	**1**	**L0, U4**
induce	8	L4, U4
🔑 inevitable	8	L4, U1
infer	7	L4, U2
infrastructure	8	L4, U10
inherent	9	L4, U5
inhibit	6	L4, U5
🔑 **initial**	**3**	**L0, U4**
initiate	6	L3, U2
🔑 injure	2	L4, U6
innovate	7	L3, U3

🔑 Oxford 3000™ words

Word	Sublist	Location
input	6	L2, U2
insert	7	L2, U7
insight	9	L3, U7
inspect	8	L4, U7
🔑 instance	3	L3, U4
🔑 institute	2	L1, U8
instruct	6	L1, U10
integral	9	L4, U5
integrate	4	L4, U7
integrity	10	L2, U8
🔑 **intelligence**	**6**	**L0, U8**
🔑 intense	8	L3, U7
interact	3	L2, U1
intermediate	9	L2, U7
🔑 internal	4	L1, U2
interpret	1	L4, U2
🔑 interval	6	L3, U7
intervene	7	L3, U4
intrinsic	10	L4, U5
🔑 invest	2	L3, U9
🔑 investigate	4	L2, U9
invoke	10	L4, U9
🔑 involve	1	L3, U10
isolate	7	L3, U4
🔑 **issue**	**1**	**L0, U6**
🔑 **item**	**2**	**L0, U5**
🔑 **job**	**4**	**L0, U3**
journal	2	L1, U9
🔑 justify	3	L3, U2
🔑 **label**	**4**	**L0, U5**
🔑 labor	1	L2, U4
🔑 layer	3	L4, U10
🔑 **lecture**	**6**	**L0, U8**
🔑 legal	1	L1, U3
legislate	1	L4, U1
levy	10	L4, U4
🔑 liberal	5	L4, U3
🔑 license	5	L3, U6
likewise	10	L3, U10
🔑 **link**	**3**	**L0, U5**
🔑 locate	3	L1, U1
🔑 logic	5	L3, U1
🔑 maintain	2	L1, U4
🔑 **major**	**1**	**L0, U2**
manipulate	8	L4, U2
manual	9	L3, U3
margin	5	L2, U4
mature	9	L2, U8

Word	Sublist	Location
maximize	3	L1, U7
mechanism	4	L3, U3
🔑 **media**	**7**	**L0, U9**
mediate	9	L3, U4
🔑 medical	5	L1, U2
🔑 medium	9	L1, U10
🔑 mental	5	L2, U10
🔑 method	1	L1, U3
migrate	6	L4, U10
🔑 military	9	L2, U9
minimal	9	L1, U8
minimize	8	L3, U9
🔑 minimum	6	L1, U8
🔑 ministry	6	L4, U1
🔑 **minor**	**3**	**L0, U8**
mode	7	L3, U2
modify	5	L1, U10
🔑 monitor	5	L3, U7
motive	6	L2, U4
mutual	9	L2, U10
negate	3	L4, U8
🔑 network	5	L2, U5
neutral	6	L2, U9
🔑 nevertheless	6	L3, U10
nonetheless	10	L4, U6
norm	9	L4, U5
🔑 **normal**	**2**	**L0, U3**
🔑 notion	5	L4, U2
notwithstanding	10	L4, U2
🔑 nuclear	8	L3, U10
🔑 **objective**	**5**	**L0, U4**
🔑 obtain	2	L3, U1
🔑 obvious	4	L1, U5
🔑 occupy	4	L4, U6
🔑 occur	1	L2, U1
🔑 odd	10	L1, U1
offset	8	L3, U2
ongoing	10	L2, U5
🔑 option	4	L1, U9
orient	5	L4, U7
outcome	3	L2, U4
🔑 output	4	L2, U3
🔑 overall	4	L2, U3
overlap	9	L2, U9
🔑 overseas	6	L3, U10
🔑 panel	10	L4, U1
paradigm	7	L4, U9
paragraph	8	L1, U1

🔑 Oxford 3000™ words

Word	Sublist	Location	Word	Sublist	Location
🔑 parallel	4	L4, U10	radical	8	L4, U2
parameter	4	L3, U8	random	8	L2, U10
🔑 participate	2	L1, U1	🔑 range	2	L2, U3
🔑 **partner**	**3**	**L0, U5**	ratio	5	L3, U6
passive	9	L3, U8	rational	6	L3, U8
perceive	2	L4, U6	🔑 react	3	L1, U5
🔑 percent	1	L1, U7	🔑 recover	6	L2, U5
🔑 period	1	L3, U4	refine	9	L3, U1
persist	10	L3, U7	regime	4	L3, U10
🔑 perspective	5	L2, U3	🔑 region	2	L3, U10
🔑 phase	4	L2, U1	🔑 register	3	L3, U9
phenomenon	7	L4, U5	regulate	2	L3, U3
🔑 philosophy	3	L3, U9	reinforce	8	L3, U6
🔑 **physical**	**3**	**L0, U1**	🔑 reject	5	L1, U10
🔑 **plus**	**8**	**L0, U6**	🔑 **relax**	**9**	**L0, U4**
🔑 policy	1	L2, U8	🔑 release	7	L1, U6
portion	9	L2, U6	🔑 relevant	2	L3, U2
🔑 pose	10	L4, U2	reluctance	10	L2, U8
🔑 **positive**	**2**	**L0, U1**	🔑 rely	3	L2, U6
🔑 potential	2	L2, U5	🔑 **remove**	**3**	**L0, U8**
practitioner	8	L4, U4	🔑 **require**	**1**	**L0, U3**
precede	6	L3, U8	🔑 **research**	**1**	**L0, U2**
🔑 precise	5	L3, U9	reside	2	L4, U4
🔑 **predict**	**4**	**L0, U3**	🔑 resolve	4	L2, U4
predominant	8	L4, U10	🔑 **resource**	**2**	**L0, U4**
preliminary	9	L2, U5	🔑 respond	1	L1, U4
presume	6	L4, U6	🔑 restore	8	L2, U5
🔑 **previous**	**2**	**L0, U5**	restrain	9	L3, U6
🔑 primary	2	L1, U4	🔑 restrict	2	L2, U6
prime	5	L4, U6	🔑 retain	4	L4, U8
🔑 principal	4	L2, U7	🔑 reveal	6	L2, U10
🔑 principle	1	L3, U8	revenue	5	L3, U9
🔑 prior	4	L2, U9	🔑 reverse	7	L3, U4
🔑 priority	7	L2, U5	🔑 revise	8	L1, U8
🔑 proceed	1	L2, U7	🔑 revolution	9	L4, U3
🔑 process	1	L1, U5	rigid	9	L2, U8
🔑 professional	4	L1, U8	🔑 **role**	**1**	**L0, U7**
prohibit	7	L3, U5	🔑 route	9	L3, U10
🔑 project	4	L1, U1			
🔑 promote	4	L4, U4	scenario	9	L2, U8
🔑 proportion	3	L2, U6	🔑 schedule	7	L1, U2
🔑 prospect	8	L4, U2	scheme	3	L4, U8
protocol	9	L4, U8	scope	6	L2, U10
psychology	5	L2, U6	🔑 **section**	**1**	**L0, U2**
🔑 publication	7	L3, U7	🔑 sector	1	L4, U9
🔑 **publish**	**3**	**L0, U10**	🔑 secure	2	L1, U4
🔑 **purchase**	**2**	**L0, U5**	🔑 seek	2	L2, U9
🔑 pursue	5	L4, U1	🔑 select	2	L1, U6
			sequence	3	L1, U6
qualitative	9	L4, U5	🔑 **series**	**4**	**L0, U2**
🔑 quote	7	L1, U9	🔑 sex	3	L4, U5

🔑 Oxford 3000™ words

Word	Sublist	Location
shift	3	L2, U7
significant	1	L3, U7
similar	1	L1, U6
simulate	7	L3, U3
site	2	L1, U1
so-called	10	L2, U1
sole	7	L4, U4
somewhat	7	L3, U5
source	1	L1, U6
specific	1	L1, U3
specify	3	L1, U9
sphere	9	L4, U2
stable	5	L3, U6
statistic	4	L2, U10
status	**4**	**L0, U9**
straightforward	10	L3, U3
strategy	2	L2, U2
stress	**4**	**L0, U1**
structure	1	L2, U7
style	5	L2, U2
submit	7	L1, U10
subordinate	9	L4, U9
subsequent	4	L3, U5
subsidy	6	L4, U3
substitute	5	L2, U6
successor	7	L3, U8
sufficient	3	L4, U1
sum	4	L3, U5
summary	4	L1, U3
supplement	9	L2, U10
survey	2	L2, U9
survive	7	L2, U8
suspend	9	L4, U1
sustain	5	L3, U6
symbol	**5**	**L0, U10**
tape	6	L3, U5
target	5	L2, U2
task	**3**	**L0, U6**
team	**9**	**L0, U1**
technical	3	L3, U6
technique	3	L3, U6
technology	3	L2, U3
temporary	**9**	**L0, U6**
tense	7	L2, U1
terminate	7	L4, U8
text	**2**	**L0, U10**
theme	7	L1, U9
theory	1	L3, U7
thereby	7	L4, U6
thesis	7	L3, U7

Word	Sublist	Location
topic	**7**	**L0, U7**
trace	6	L4, U10
tradition	**2**	**L0, U9**
transfer	2	L1, U6
transform	6	L3, U1
transit	5	L2, U2
transmit	7	L4, U10
transport	6	L1, U8
trend	5	L1, U3
trigger	9	L4, U4
ultimate	7	L3, U9
undergo	10	L4, U4
underlie	6	L4, U5
undertake	4	L4, U3
uniform	7	L2, U10
unify	9	L2, U9
unique	7	L2, U7
utilize	6	L3, U6
valid	3	L3, U8
vary	1	L1, U2
vehicle	7	L2, U2
version	5	L1, U9
via	7	L4, U3
violate	9	L3, U6
virtual	8	L3, U5
visible	**7**	**L0, U2**
vision	9	L2, U2
visual	8	L2, U7
volume	3	L1, U7
voluntary	7	L3, U4
welfare	5	L4, U4
whereas	5	L4, U5
whereby	10	L4, U8
widespread	7	L3, U4

🔑 Oxford 3000™ words